Preview Page

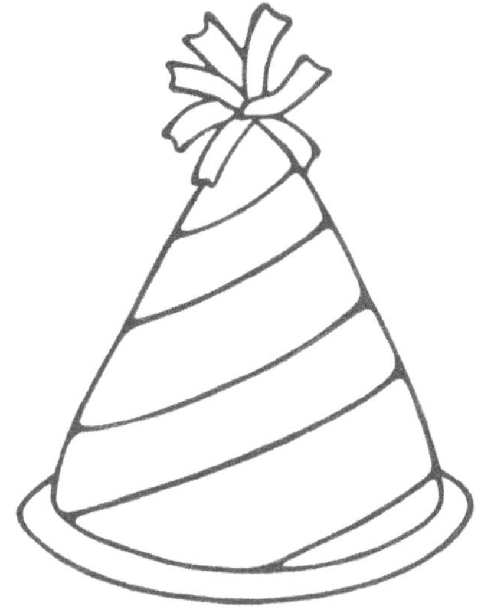

New Years ________ Party Hat

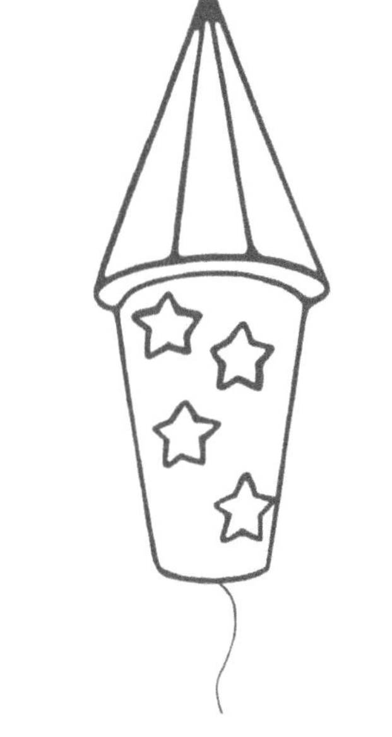

Fourth Of July __________

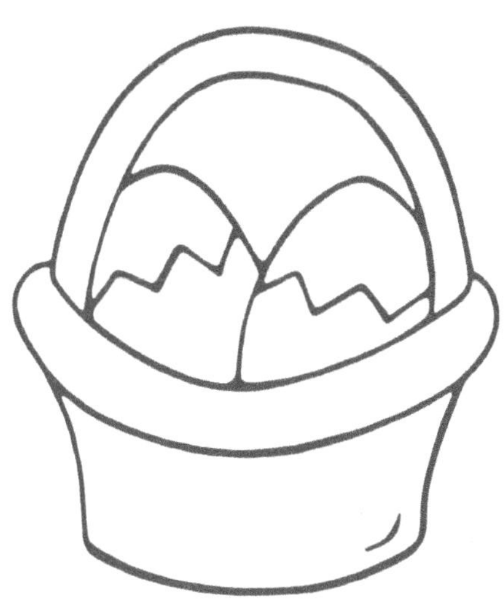

Easter ________ Basket

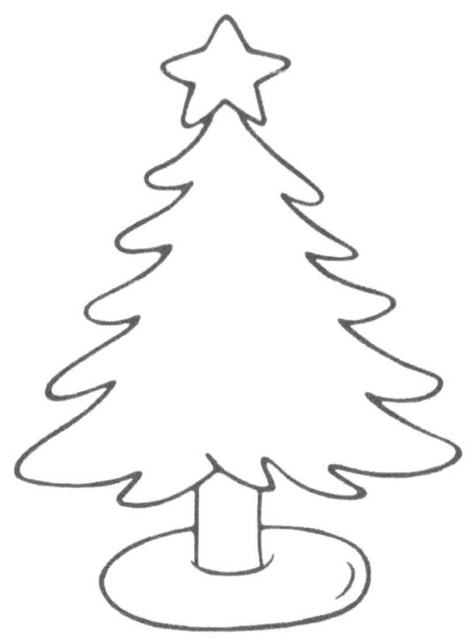

Hang _______ On The Christmas Tree

Remembering The Holidays

Book 1 of 3

This Coloring Book Is Designed With Simple Familiar Black-Line Drawings
With Sentence Cuing Common Prases For Cognitive Art Therapy - For All Ages .
Recommended At Home One On One, With A Caregiver Or Family Member
And As A Resource For Therapeutic Recreation Departments.

30 Single Sided Coloring Pages, Plus
20 Keepsake Year-Round Holiday Inspired Journal Pages

The Adult Coloring Book Craze Is Here.

Bonnie has created a great activities resource that can be used individually
on a one on one basis or in a group setting. It's simple familiar designs,
color-cuing and common phrases allow for successful completion.
Providing a positive, calm and fun experience.
I highly recommend it's use with anyone with cognitive impairment.
Every therapeutic recreation department should utilize this amazing
resource as they will immediately see the denefits.
Recommended By; Alexis Chiucarello, Director Of Therapeutic Recreation
And Dementia Program Coordinator Long Term Center.

Illustrator and Author: Bonnie S. MacLachlan

Publisher: Art.Z illustrations
Griswold, Ct
ArtZillustrations.com

Special Thanks To: Alexis Chiucarello

Made In America

Art.Z illustrations
ISBN-13: 978-09977889-1-4
ISBN-10: 0997788917

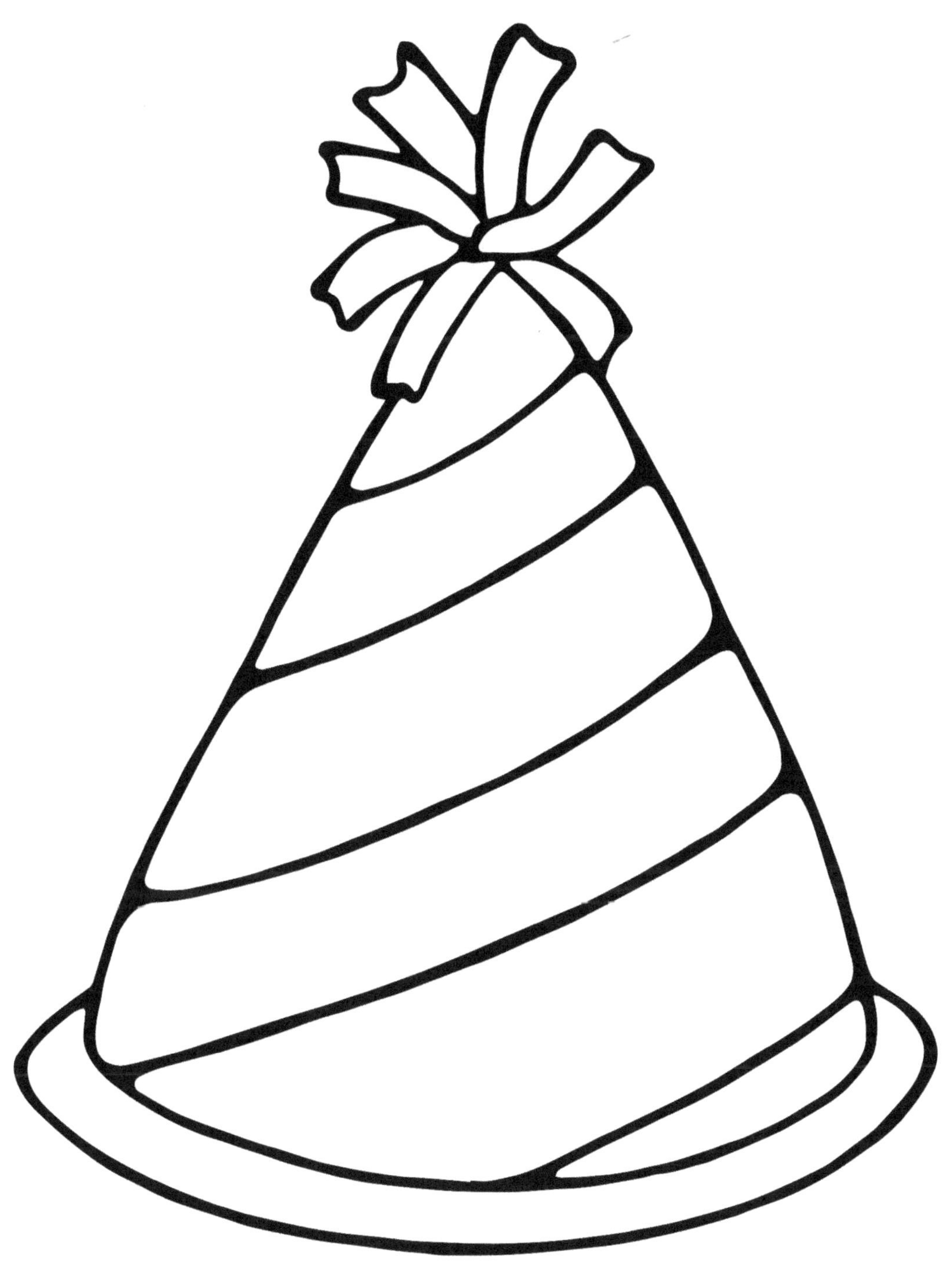

New Years __________ Party Hat

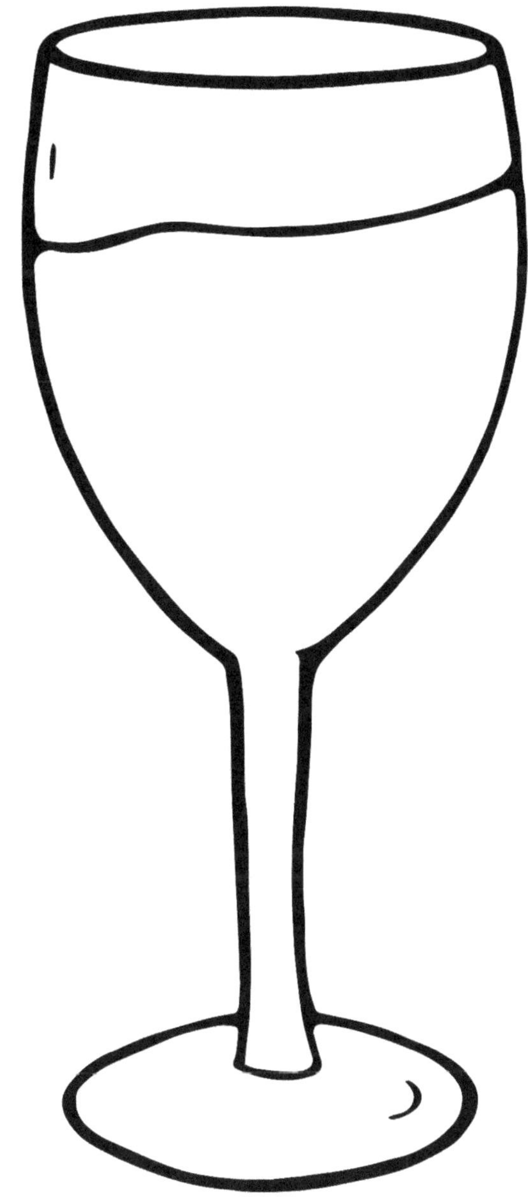

Tall Glass Of __________

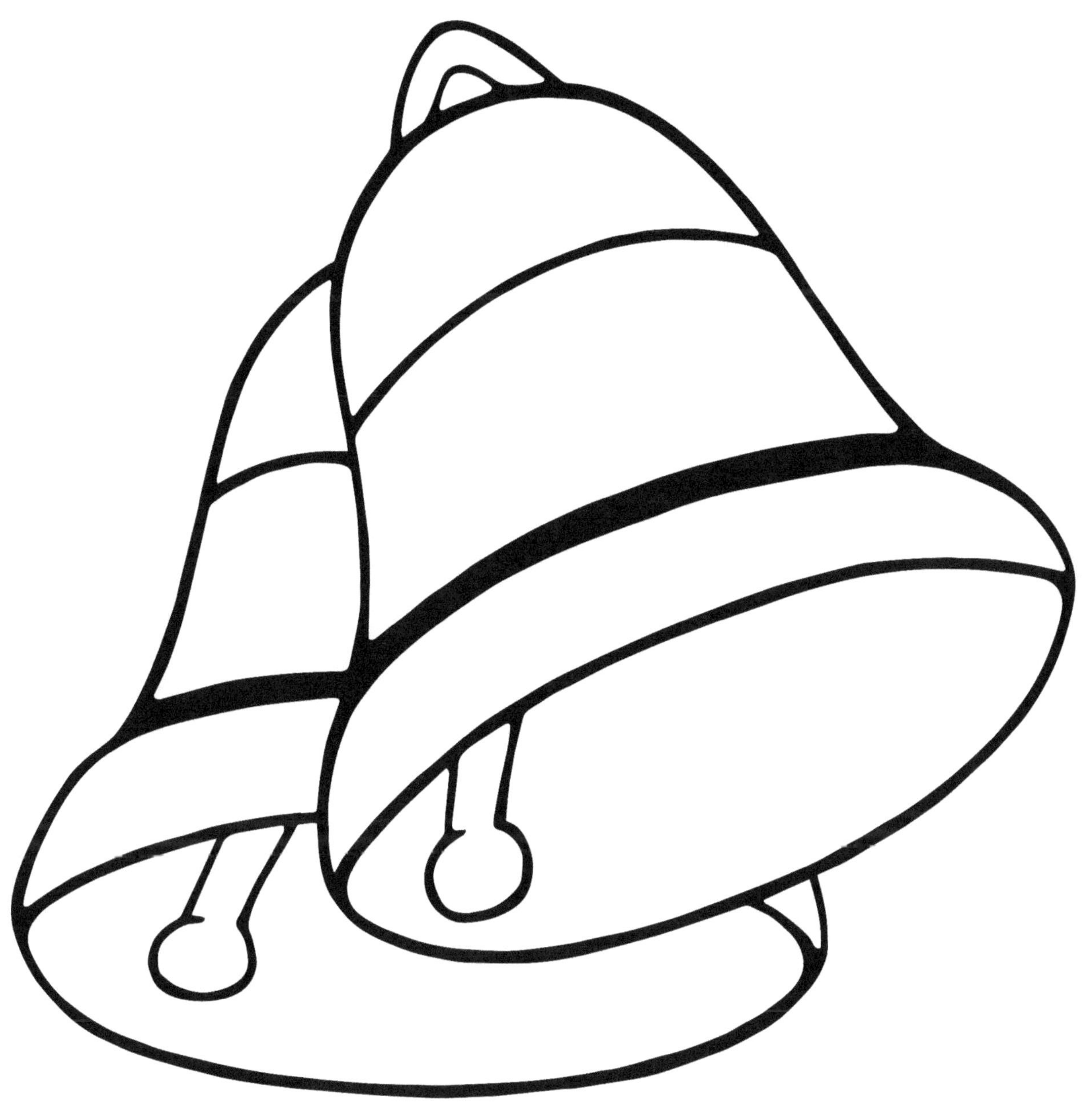

Ring In The New ___________

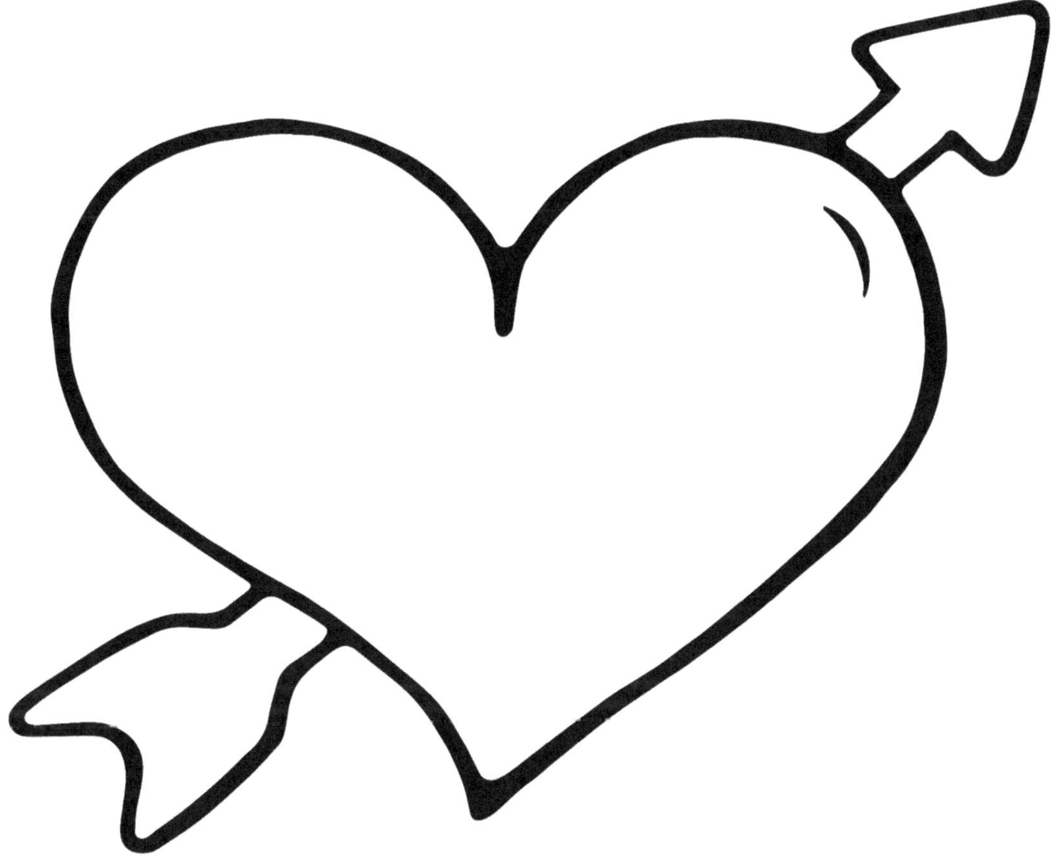

My Heart ______________

To ______________

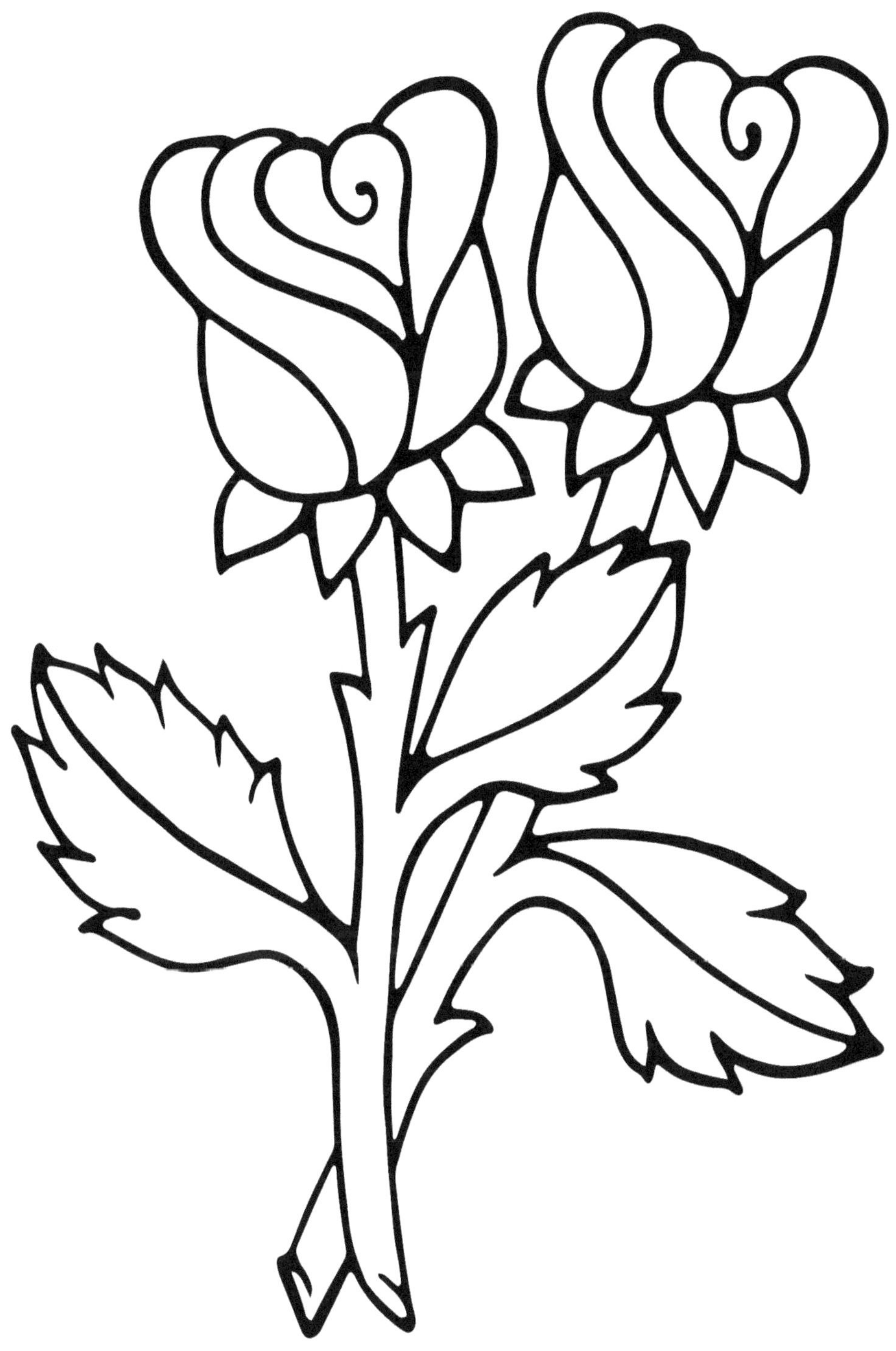

Roses Are ___________

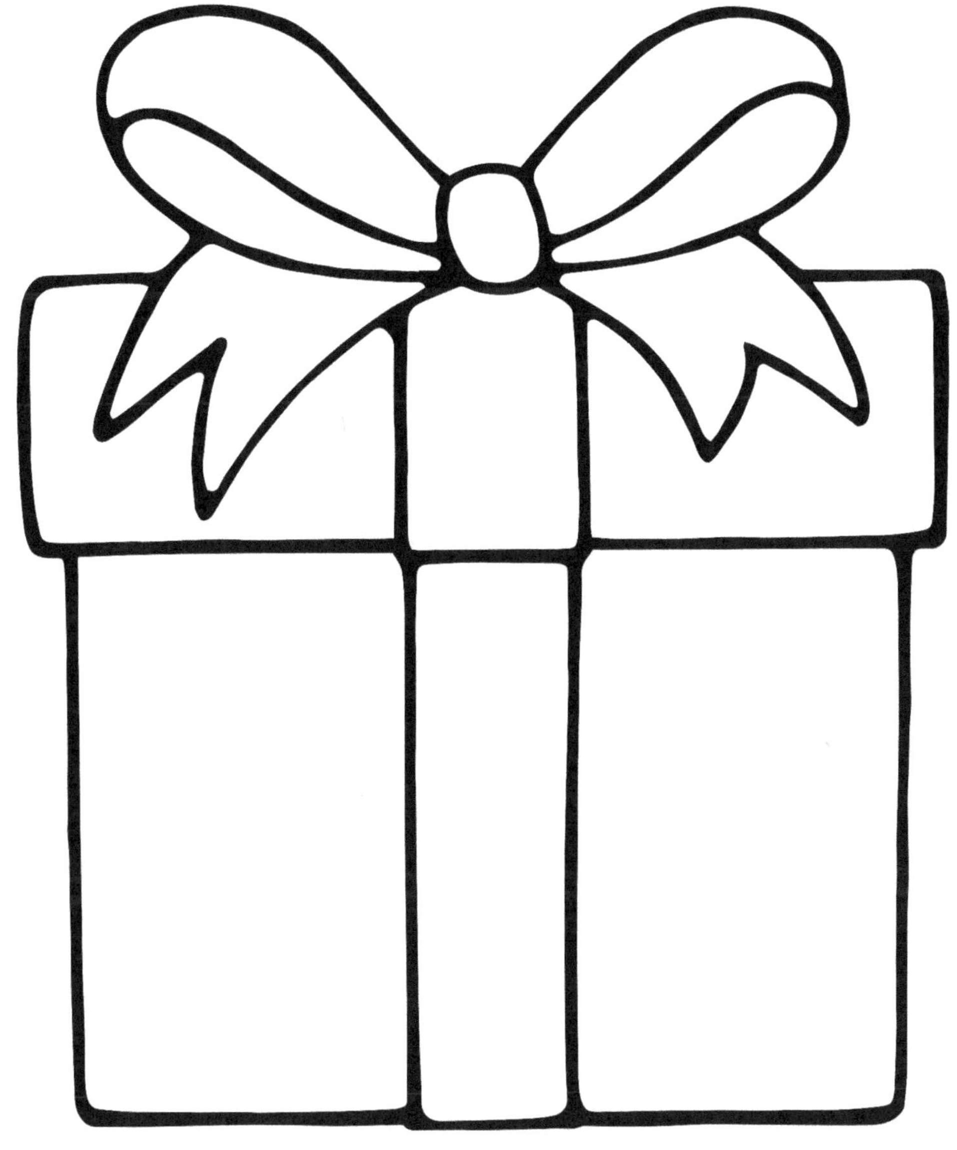

Every ____________ Is A Gift

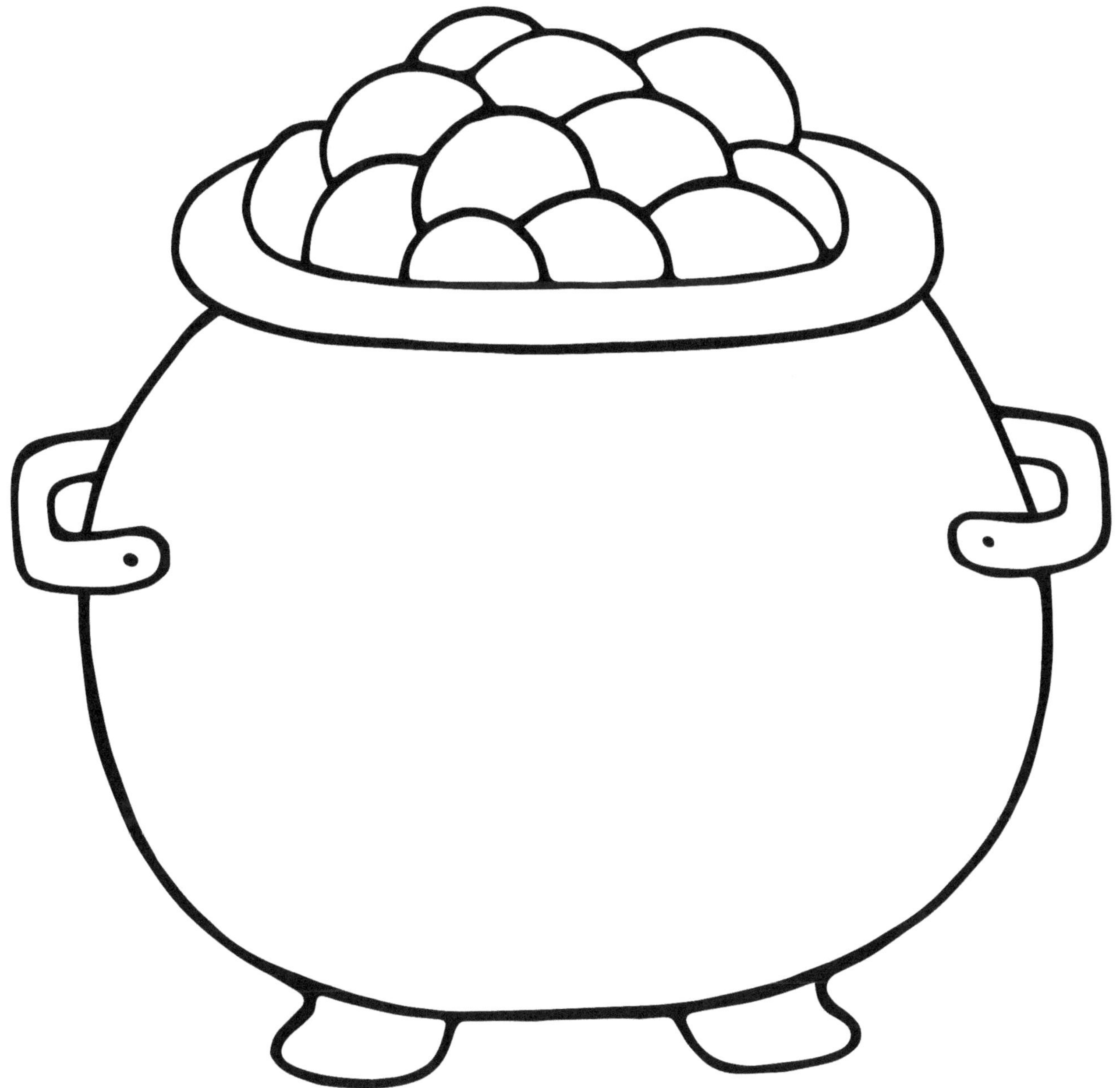

A Pot Of ___________

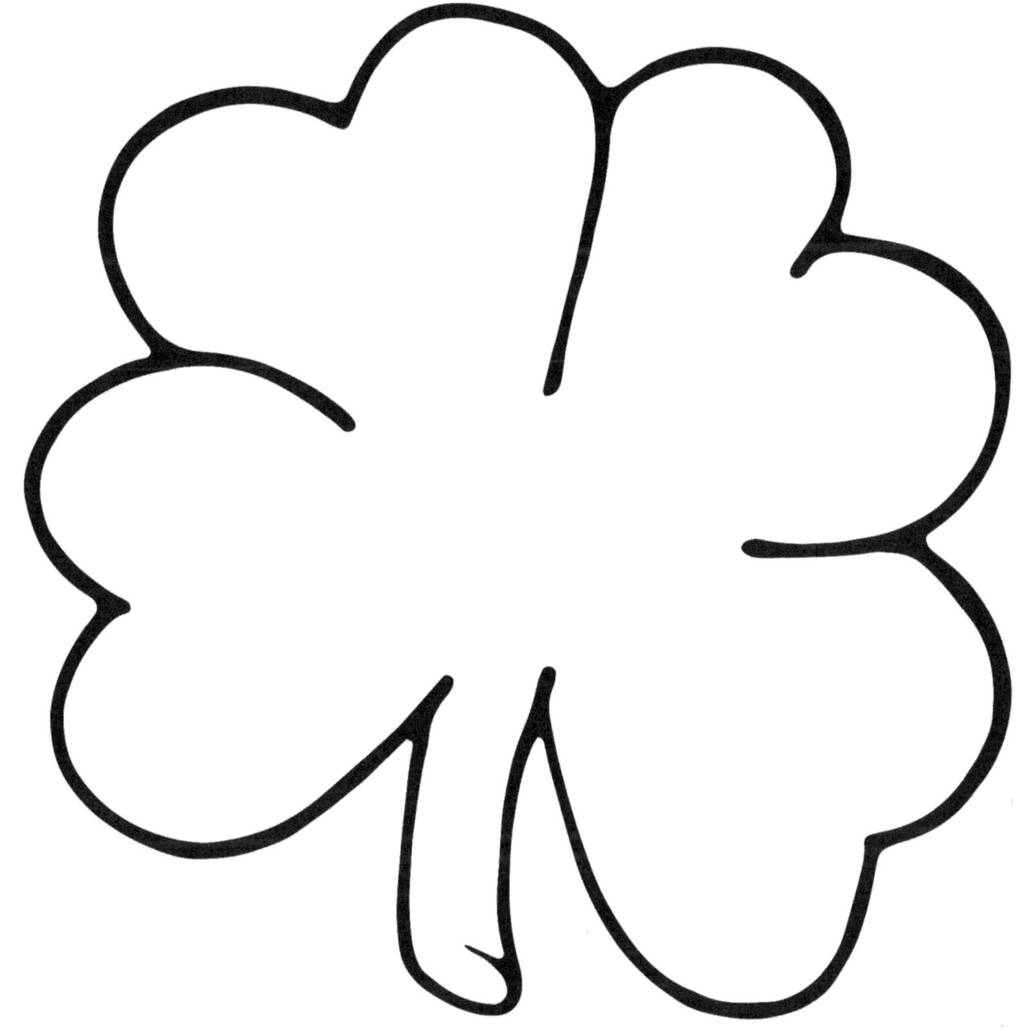

__________ Looking Over

A Four ____________ Clover

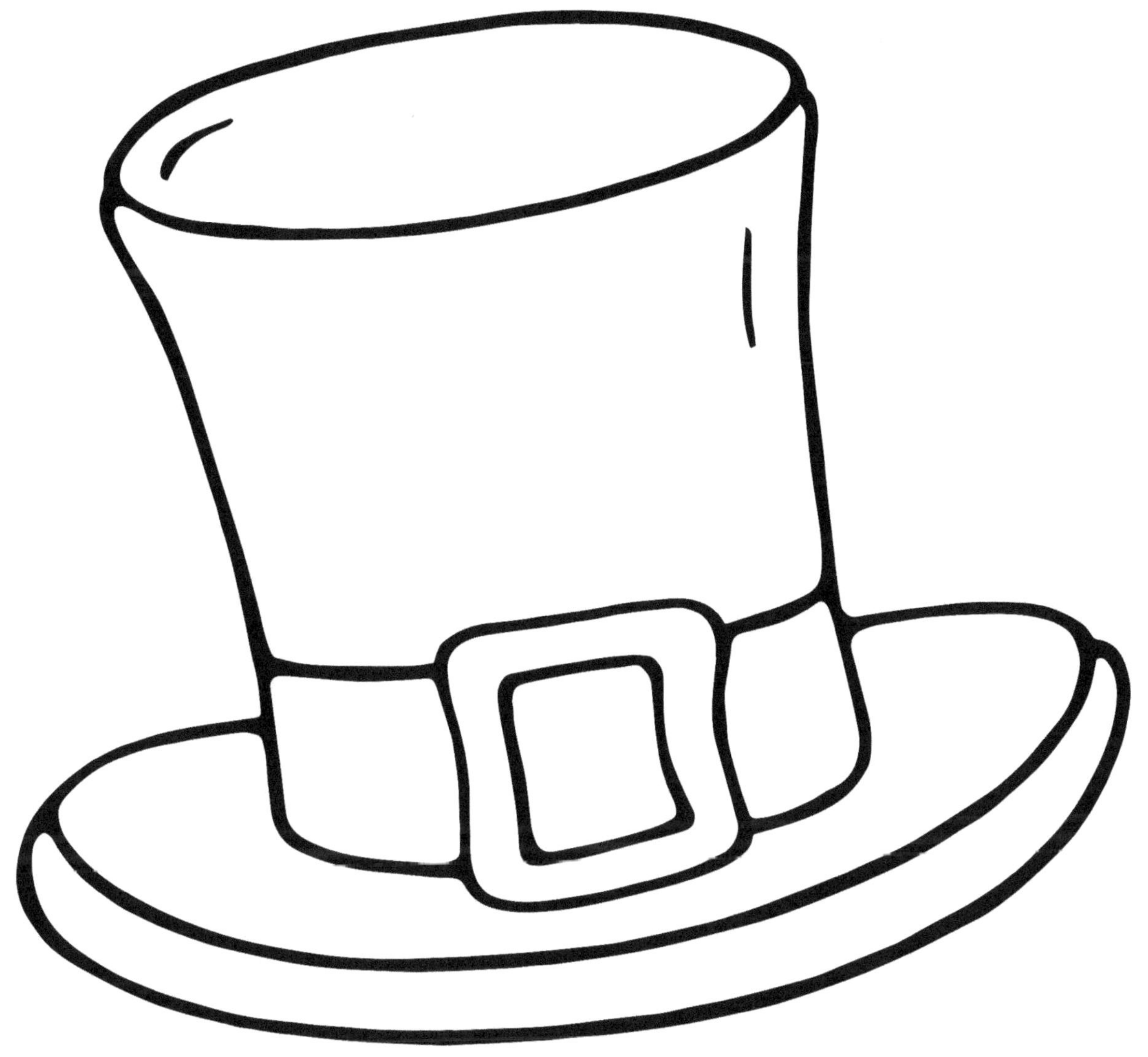

St Patricks ______________ Hat

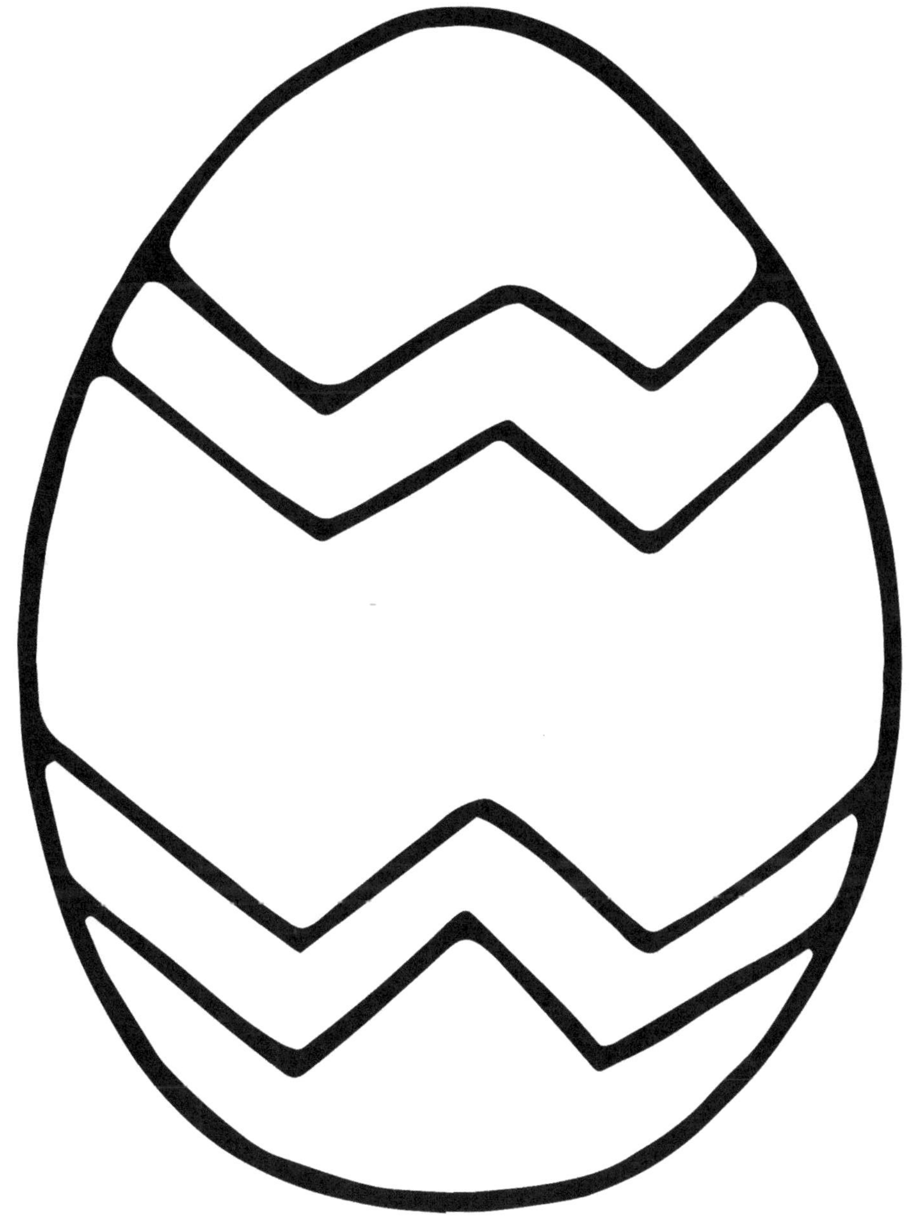

Coloring Eggs For ___________

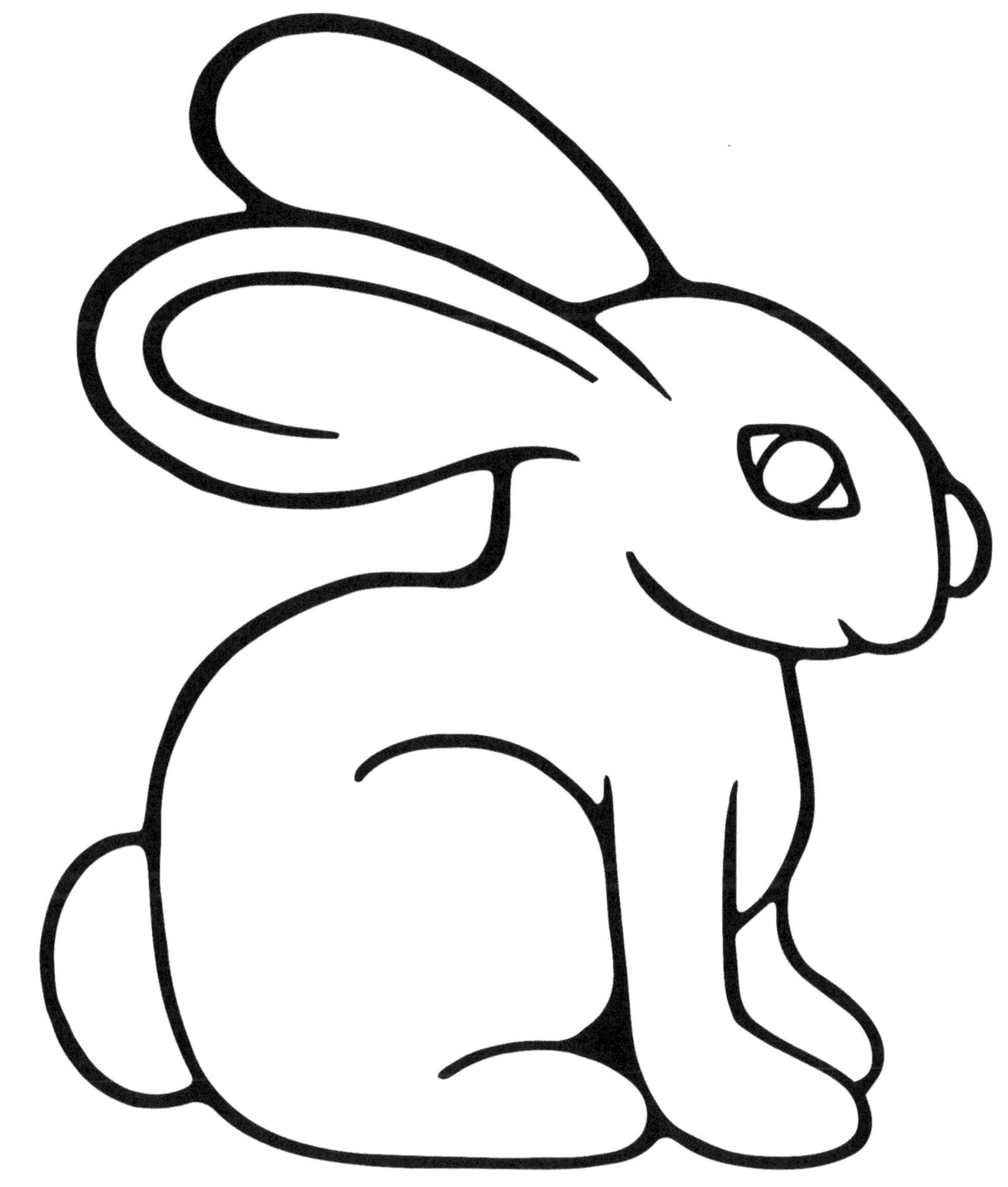

________________ Easter Rabbit

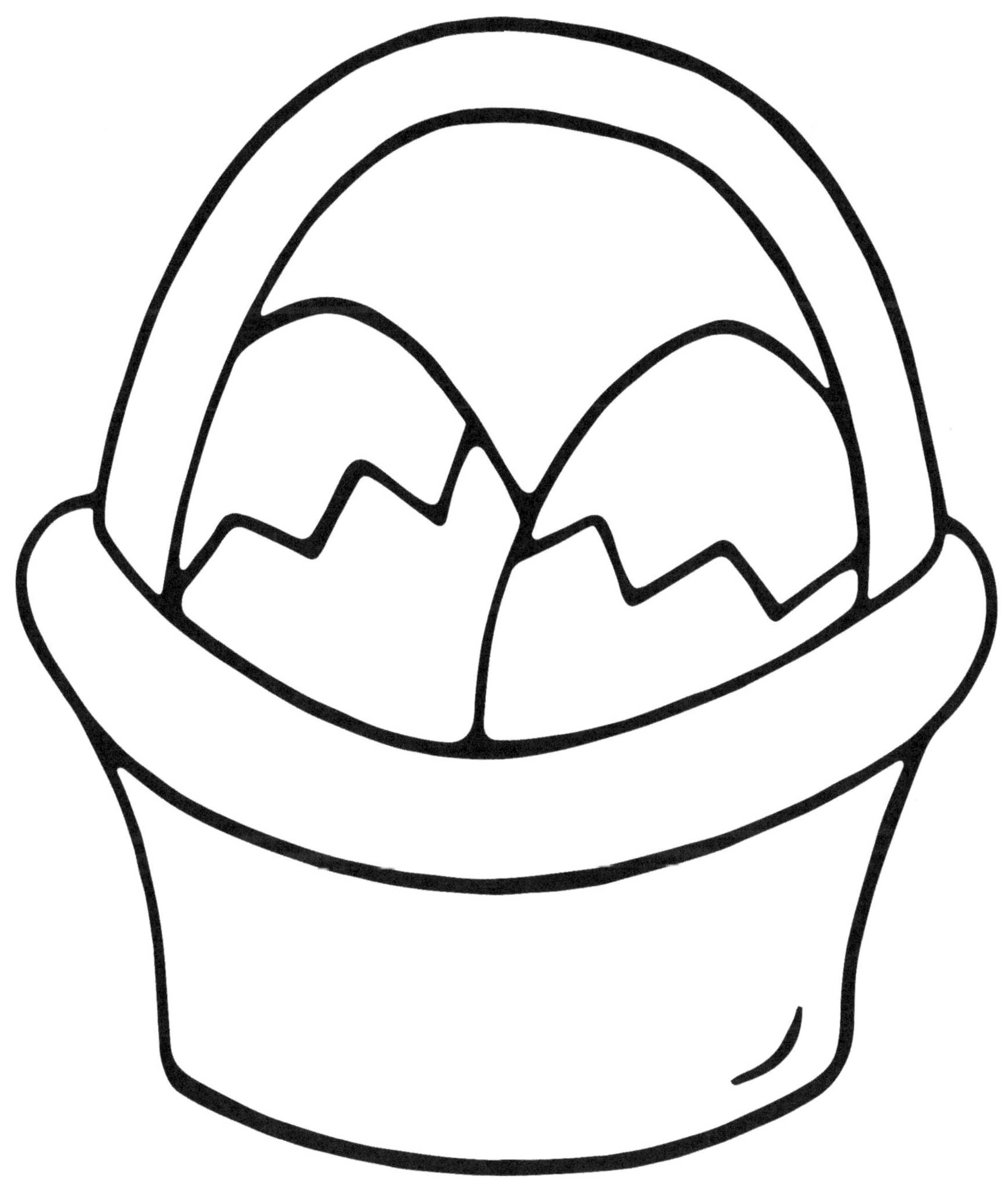

Easter ____________ Basket

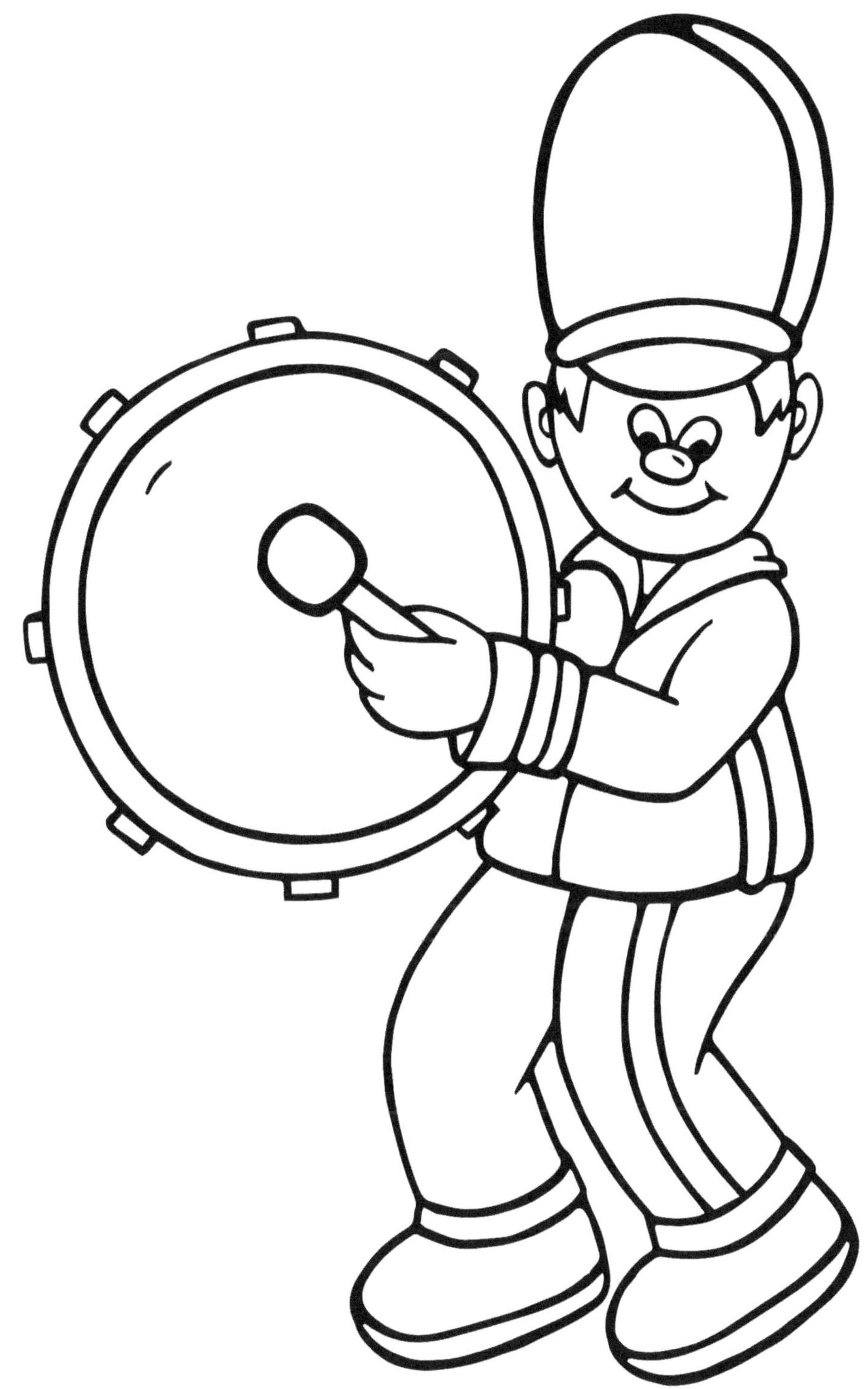

Drumming In The ___________ Parade

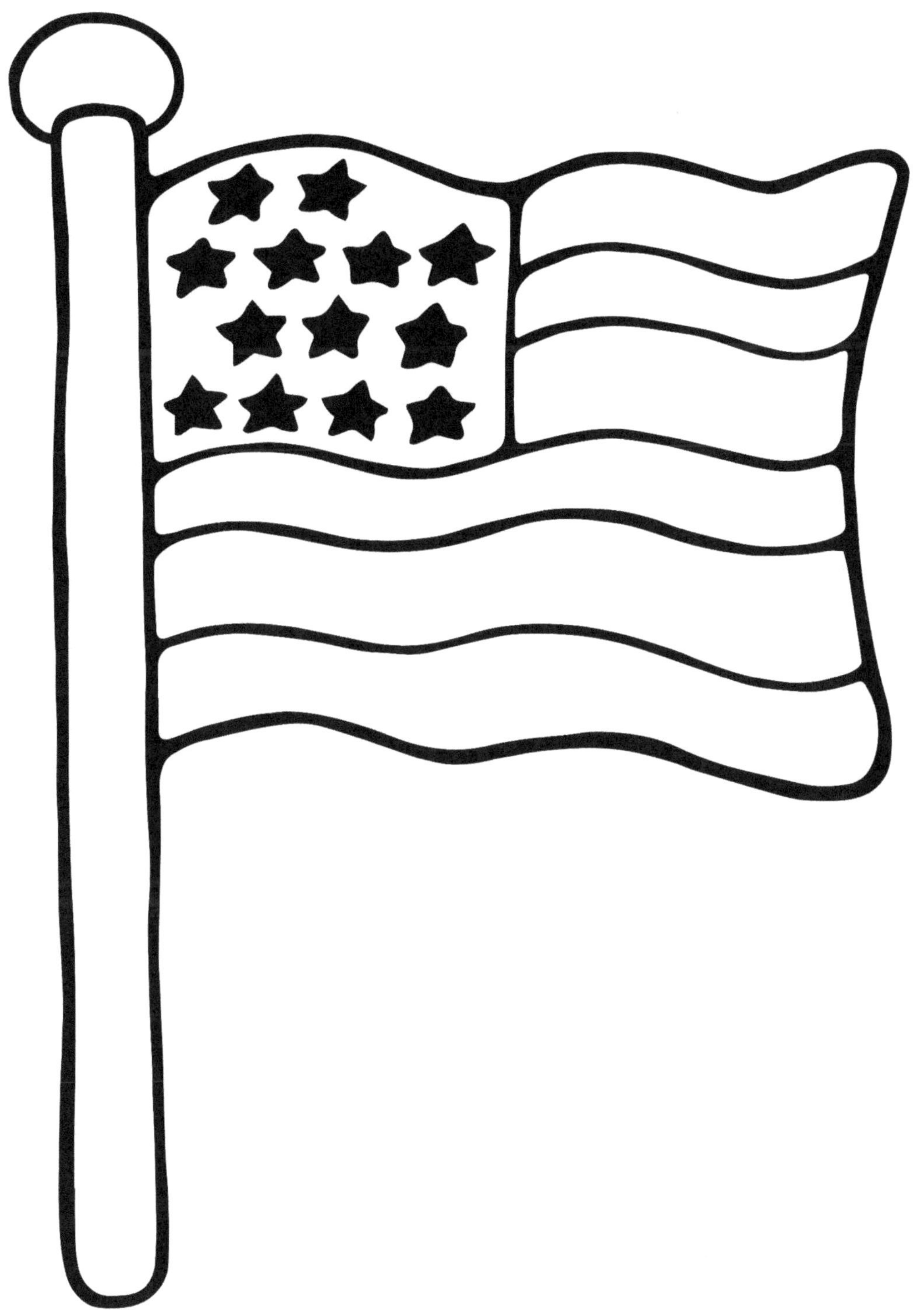

Wave The ____________ Flag

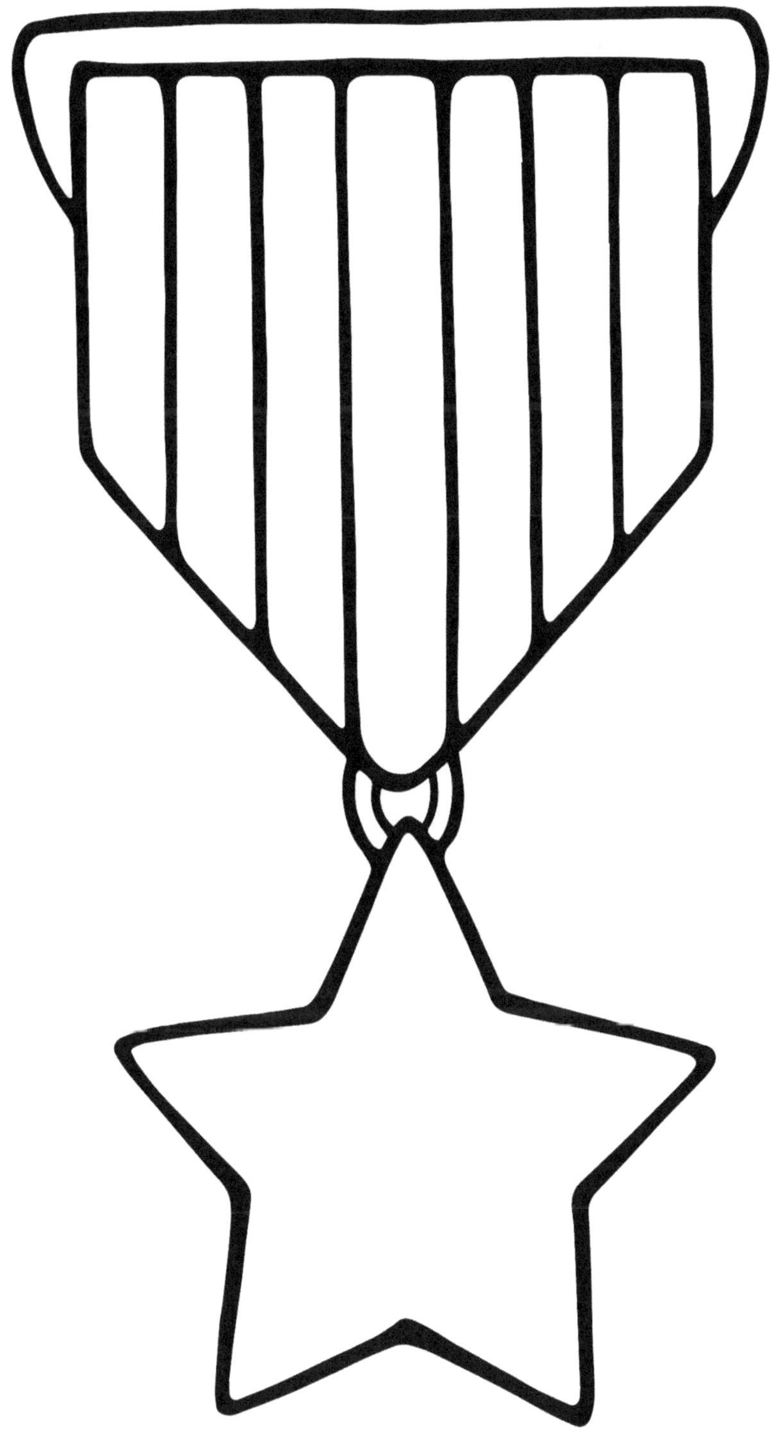

Thank ____________ Who Served

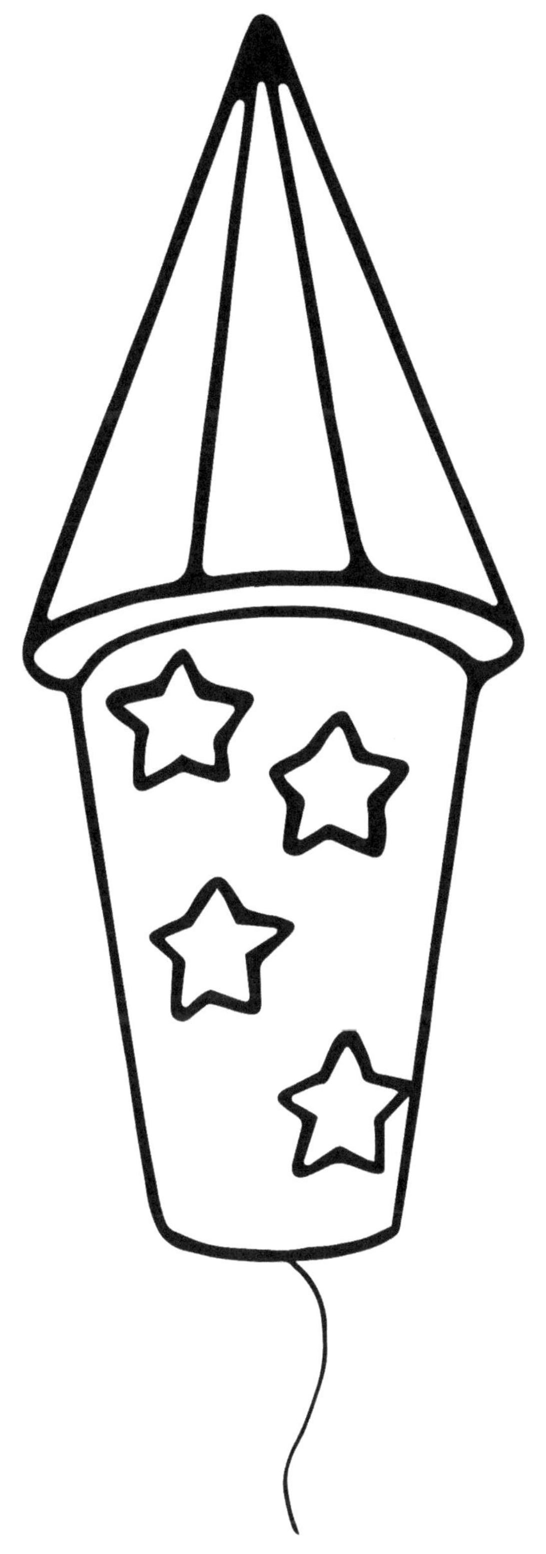

Fourth Of July ___________

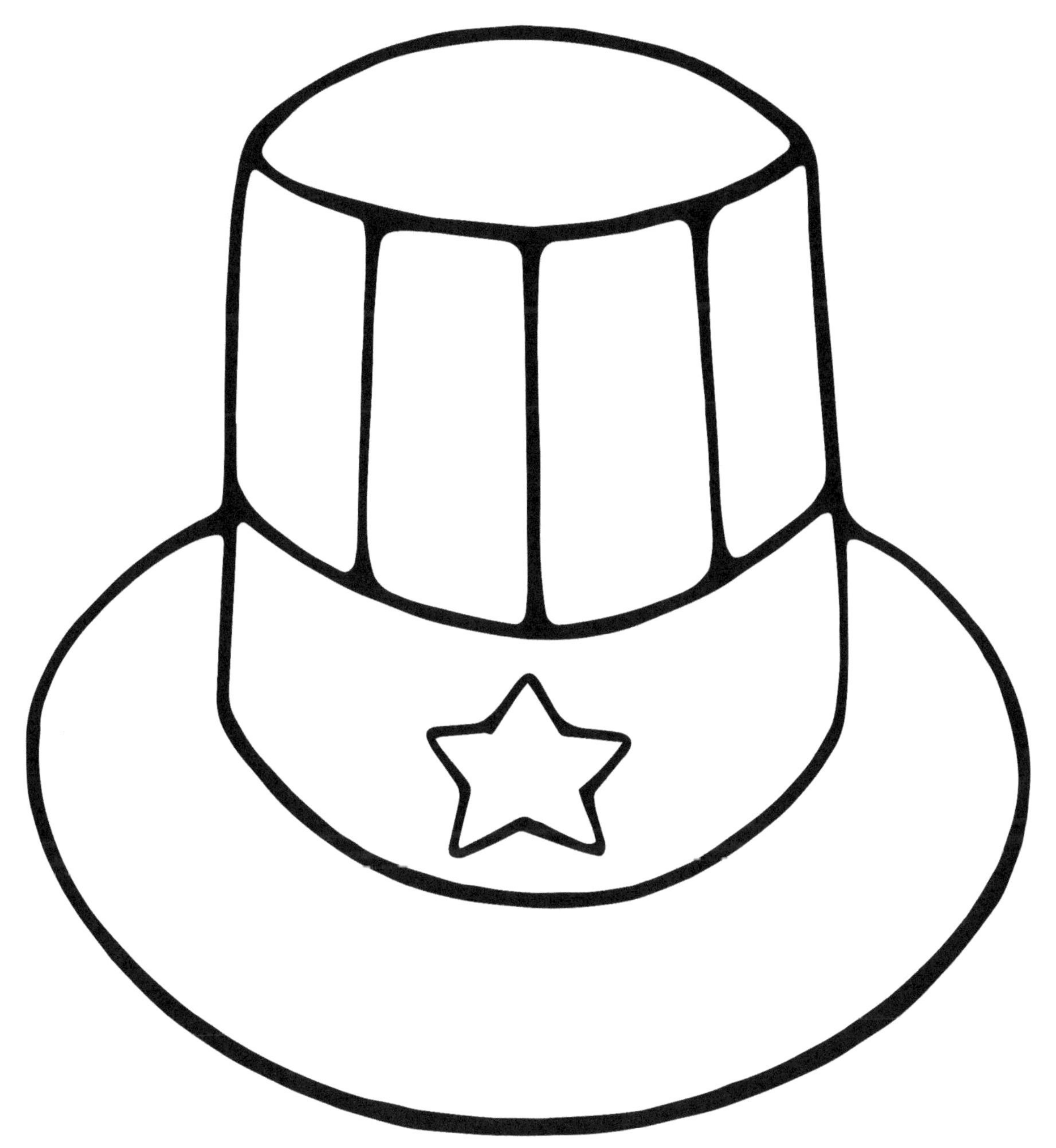

Red, White And ___________ Hat

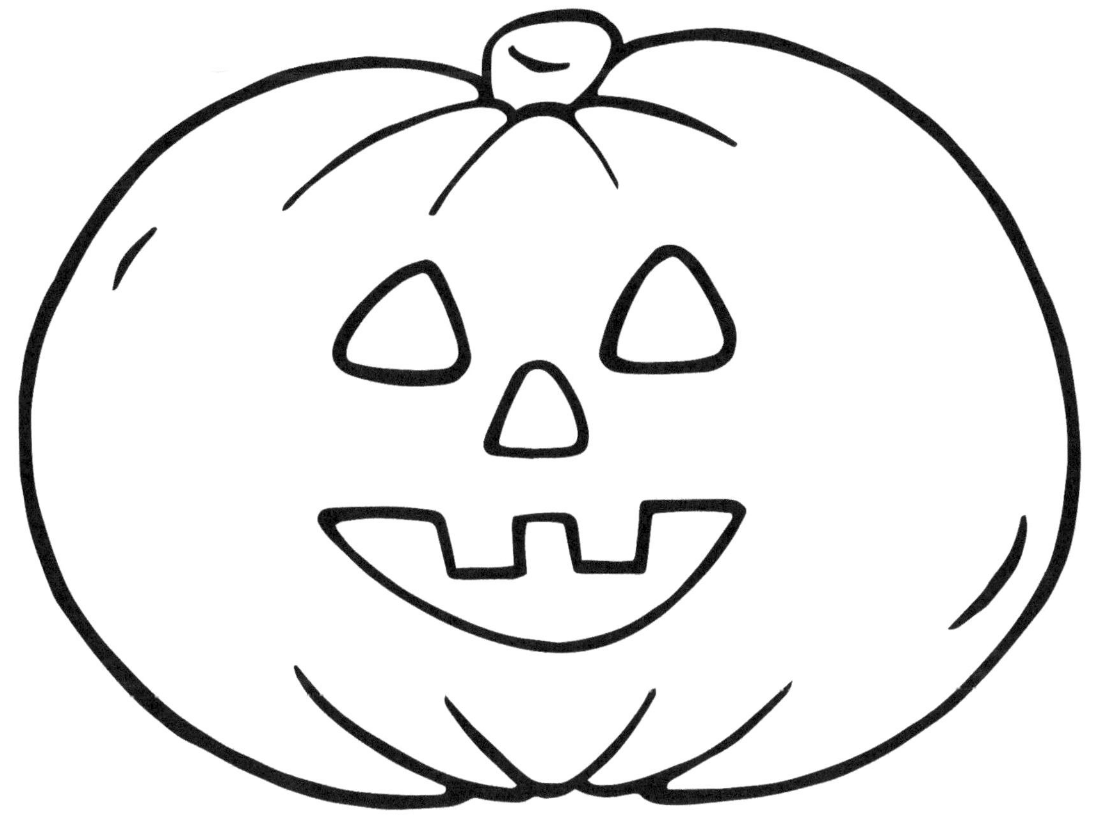

Carve A Pumpkin For___________

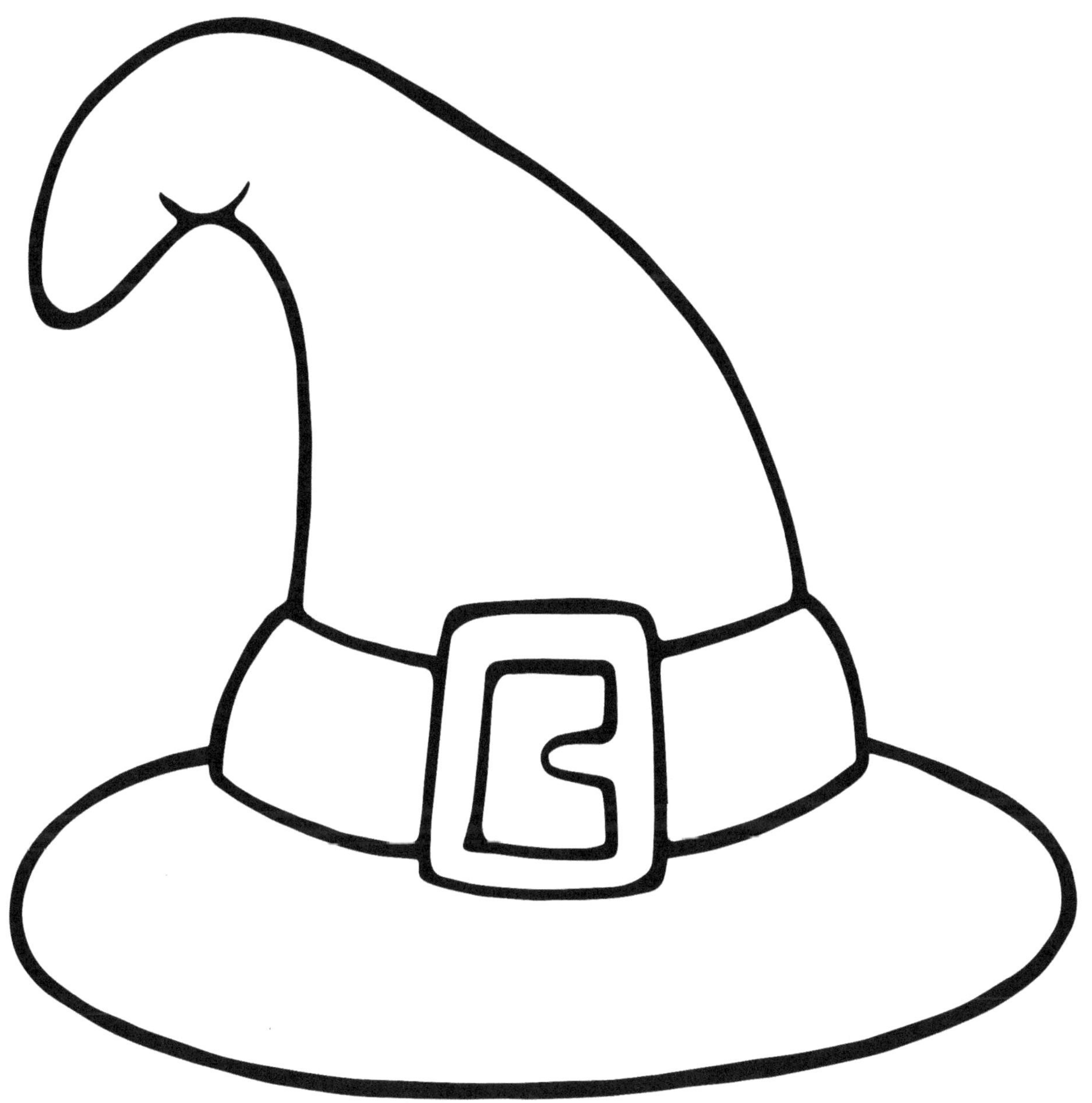

______________ Hat

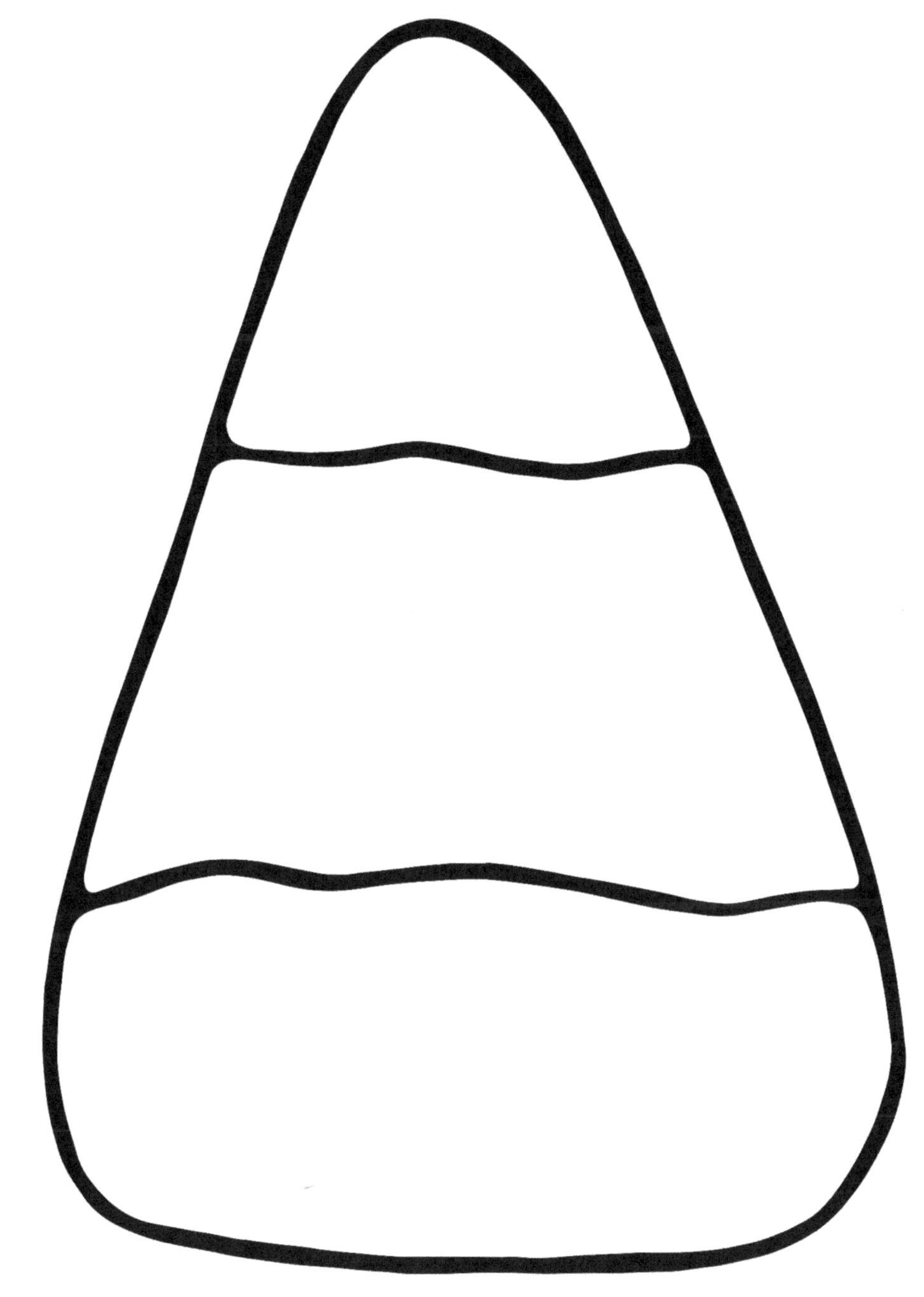

________________ Candy Corn

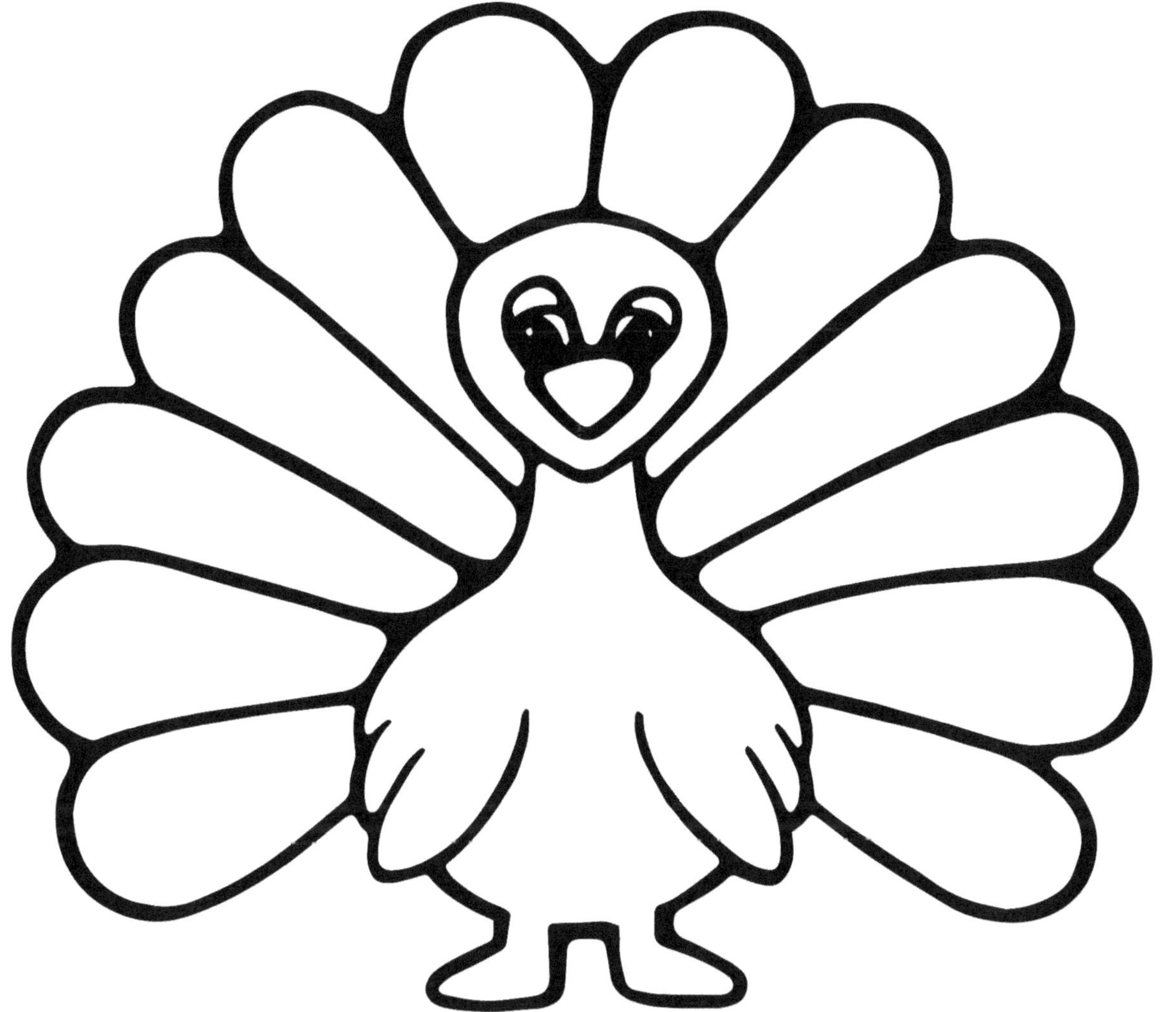

____________ Turkey

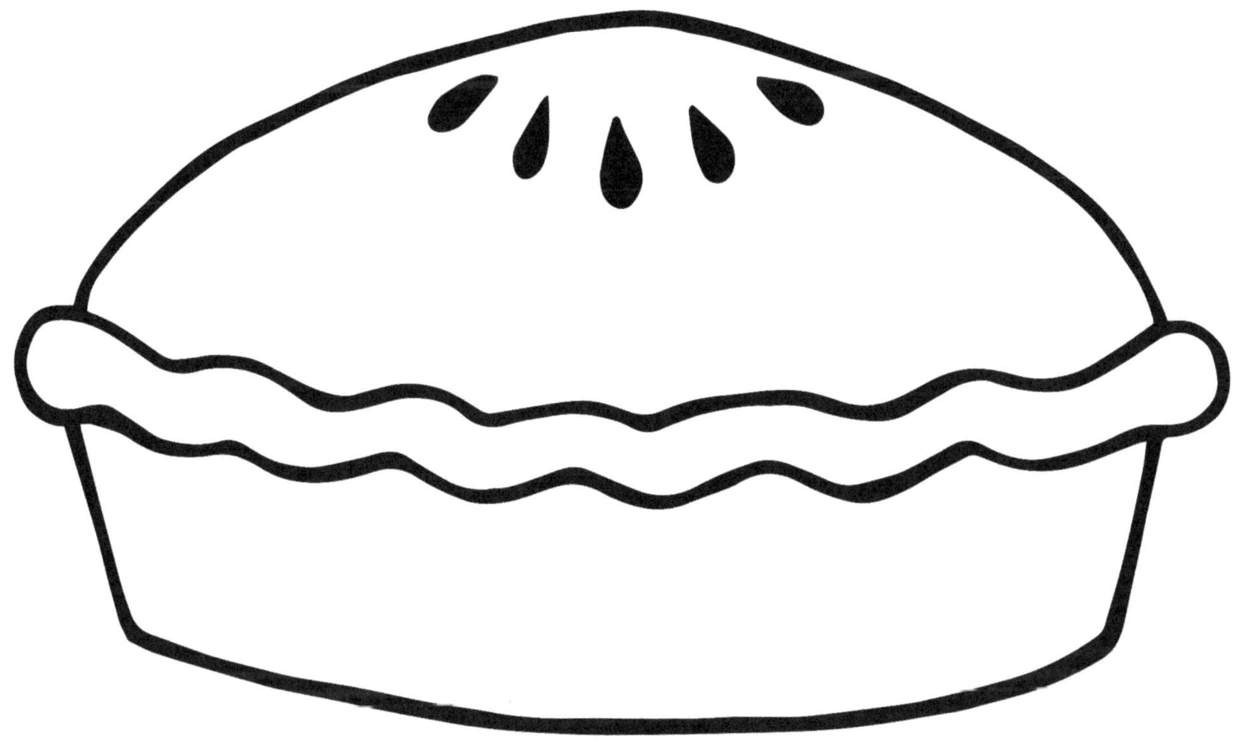

__________ Pie And __________

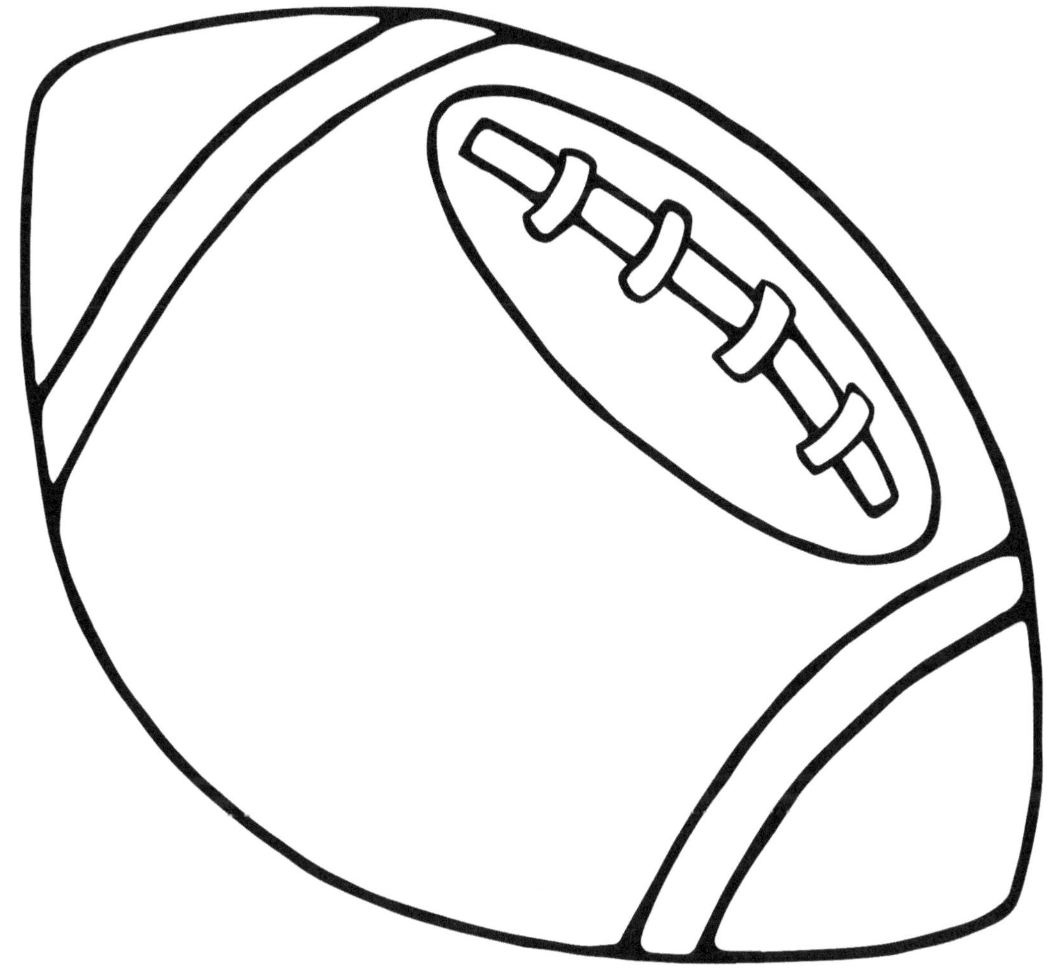

Football ___________

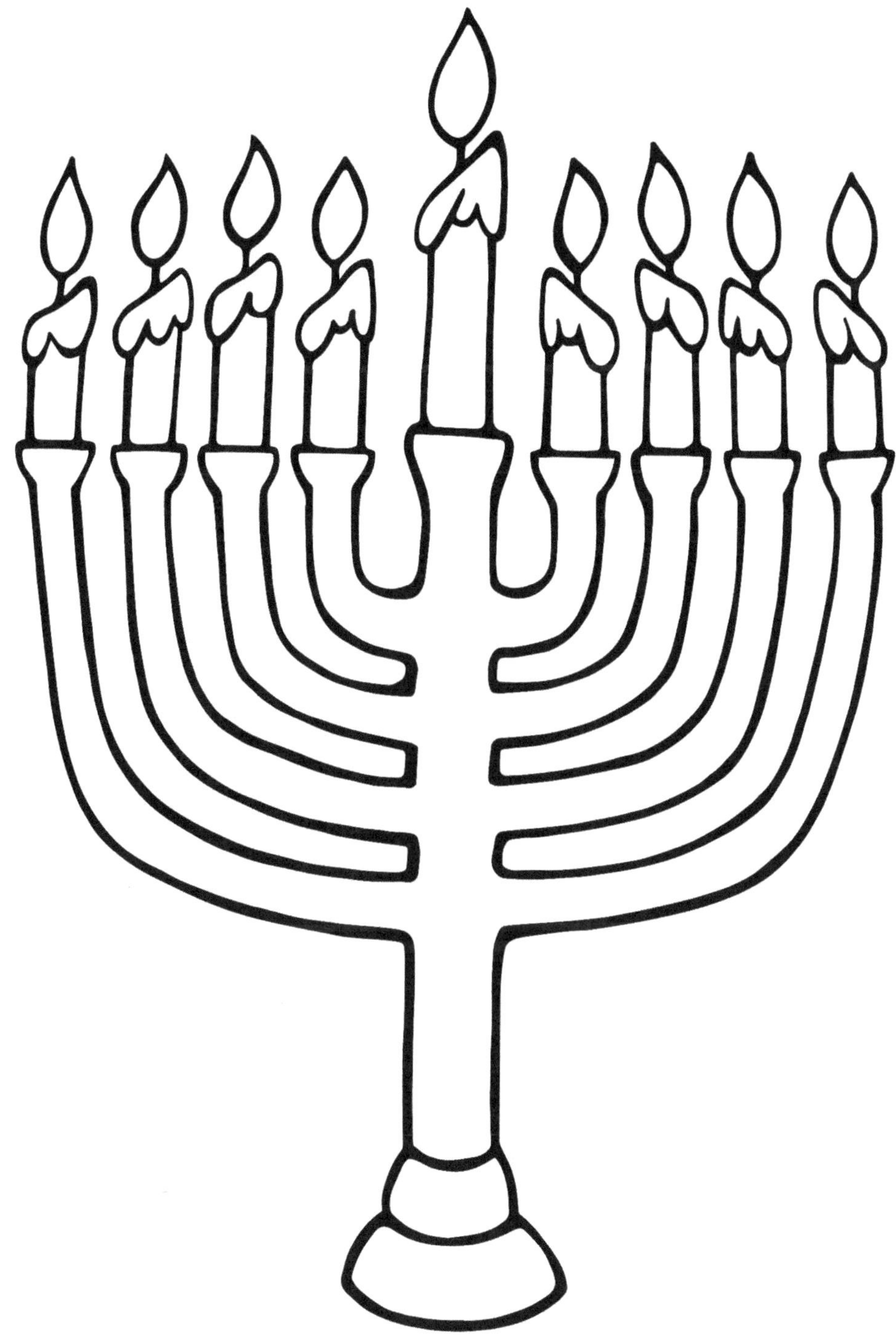

Light The Menorah For ___________

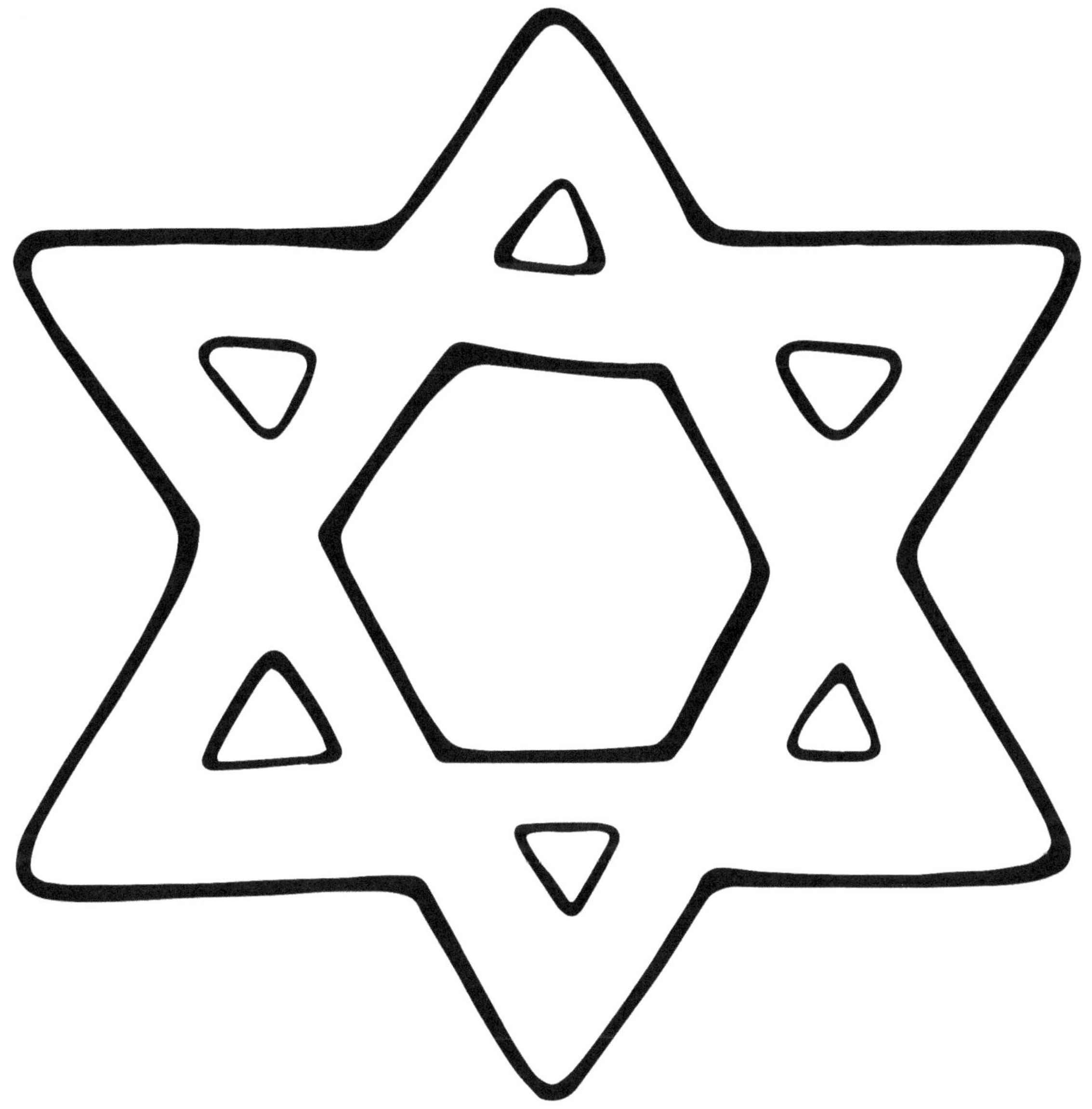

Star Of __________

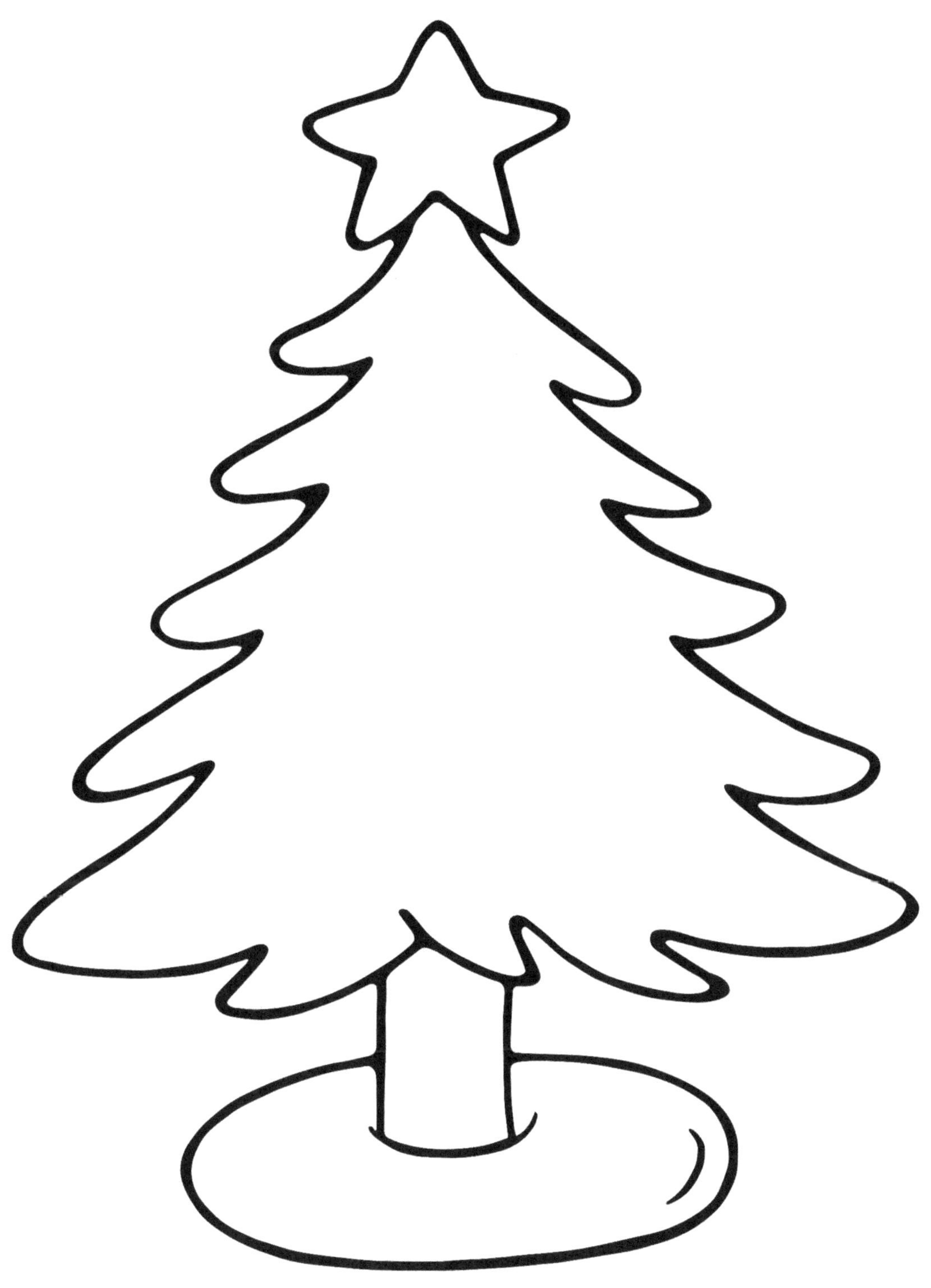

Hang __________ On The Christmas Tree

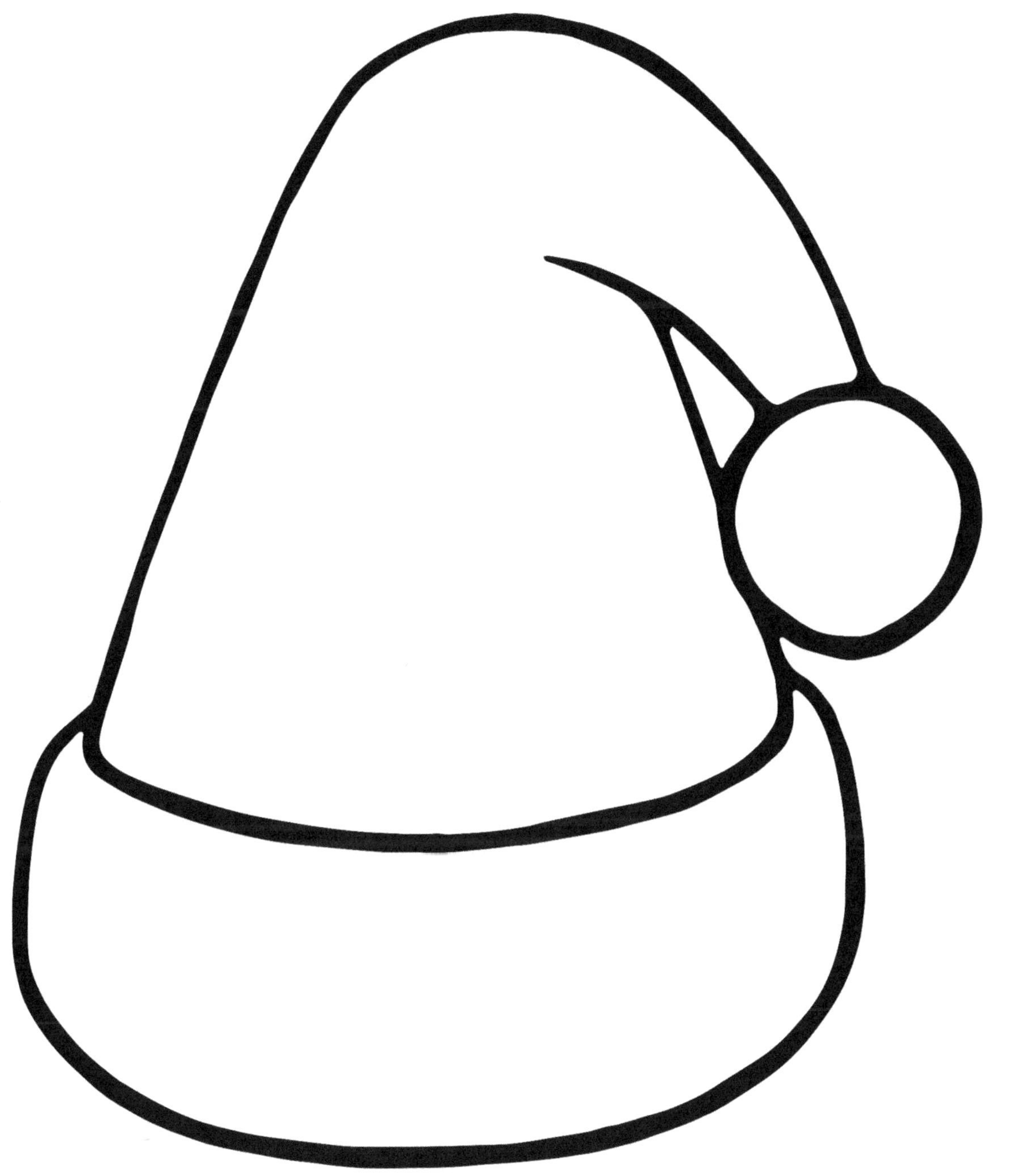

Santa's ___________ Hat

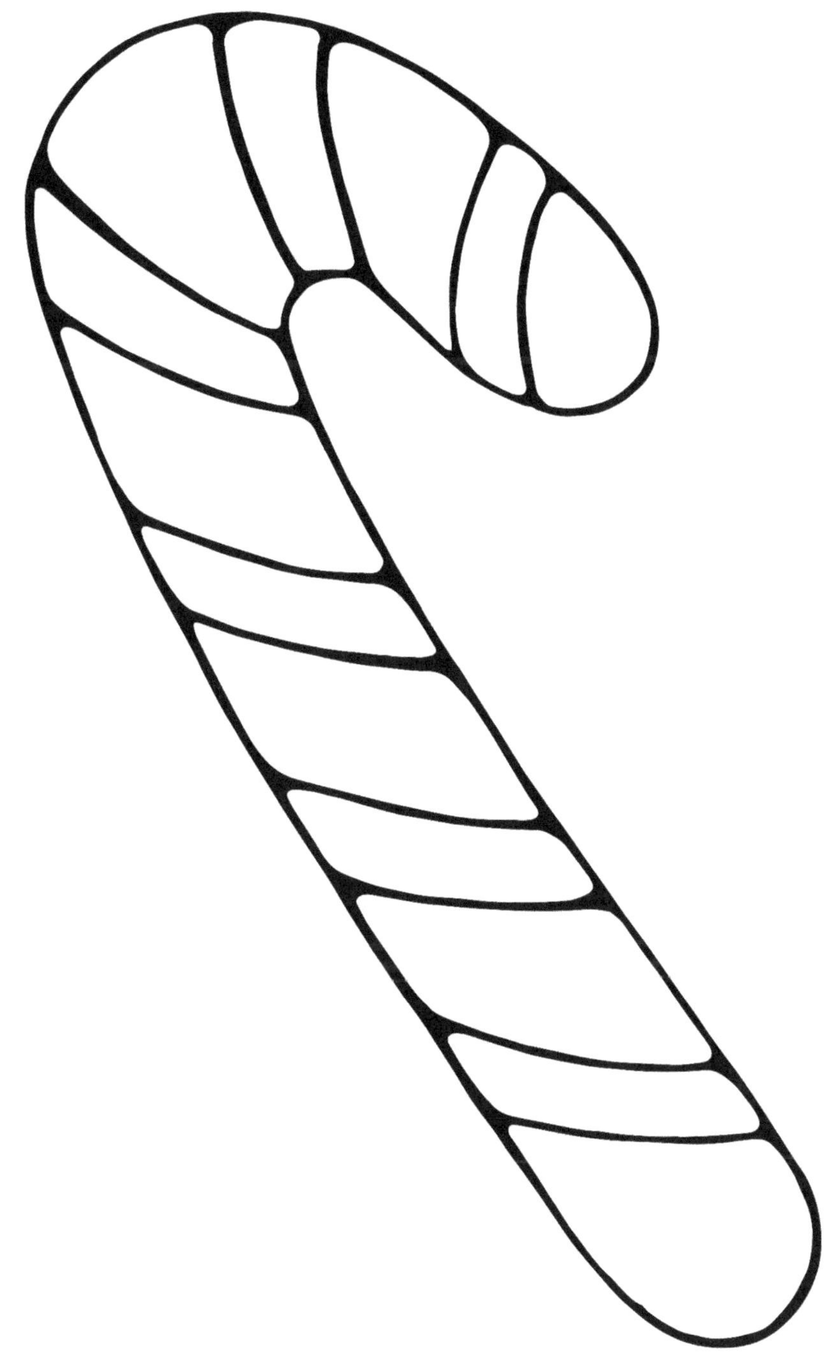

_______________ Candy Canes

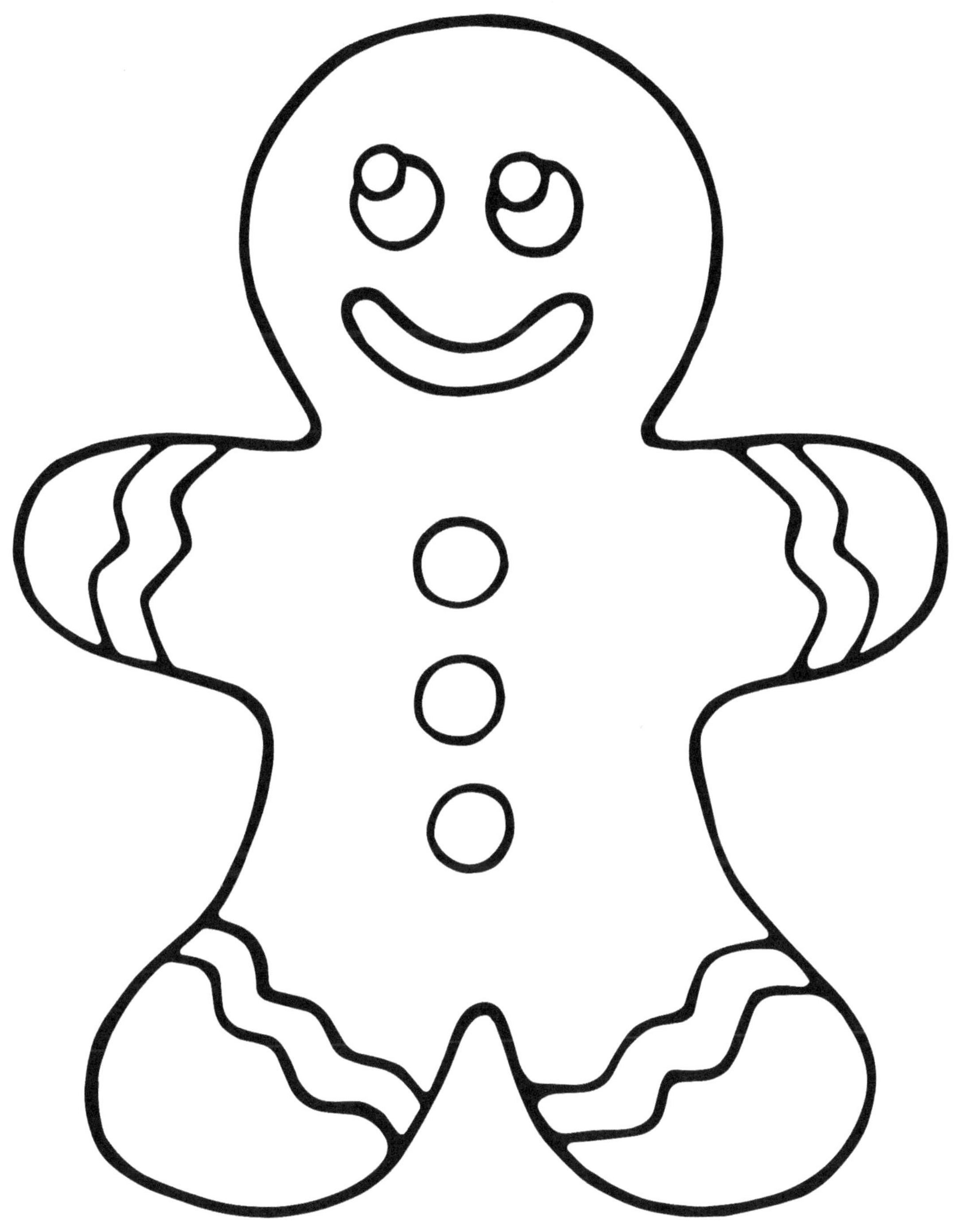

Gingerbread ____________

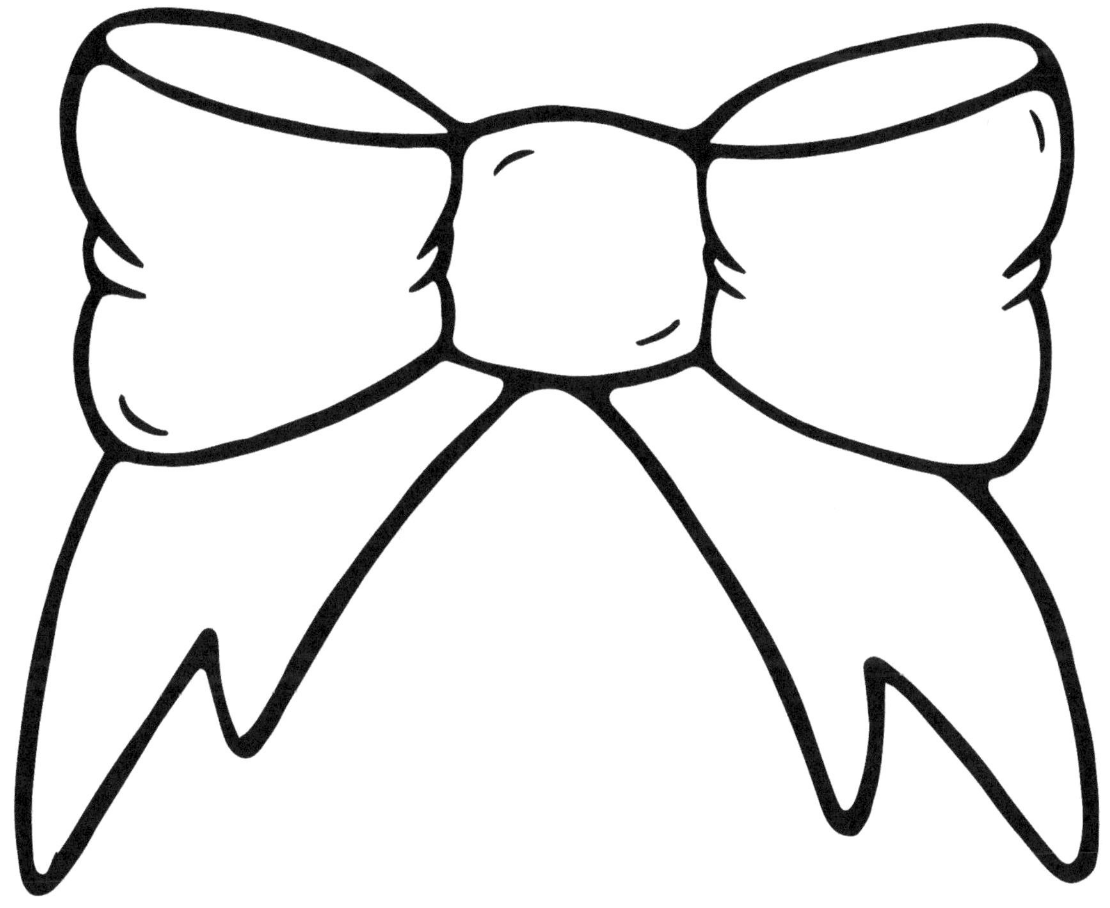

Tie A Present With A Big ___________

Holiday Journal Pages

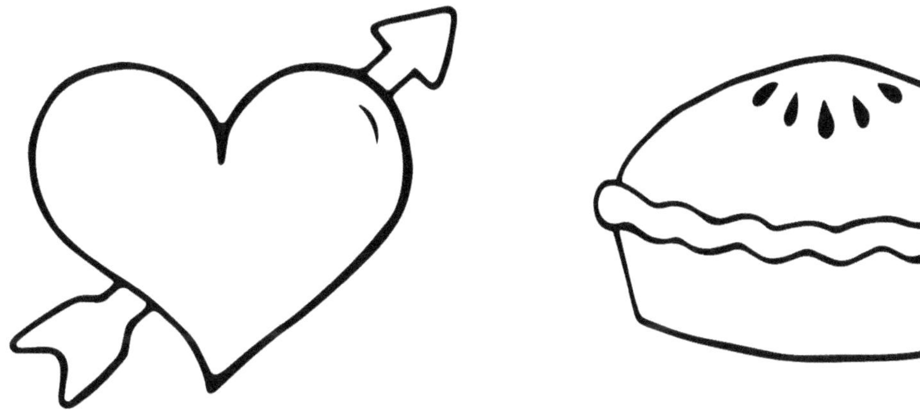

As you go through the pages of this book, Sweet, Fun and Loving Holiday Stories with Family and Friends will Inevitably be Remembered.

Use the following pages, to keep record of these precious memories, to prevent them from being lost forever.

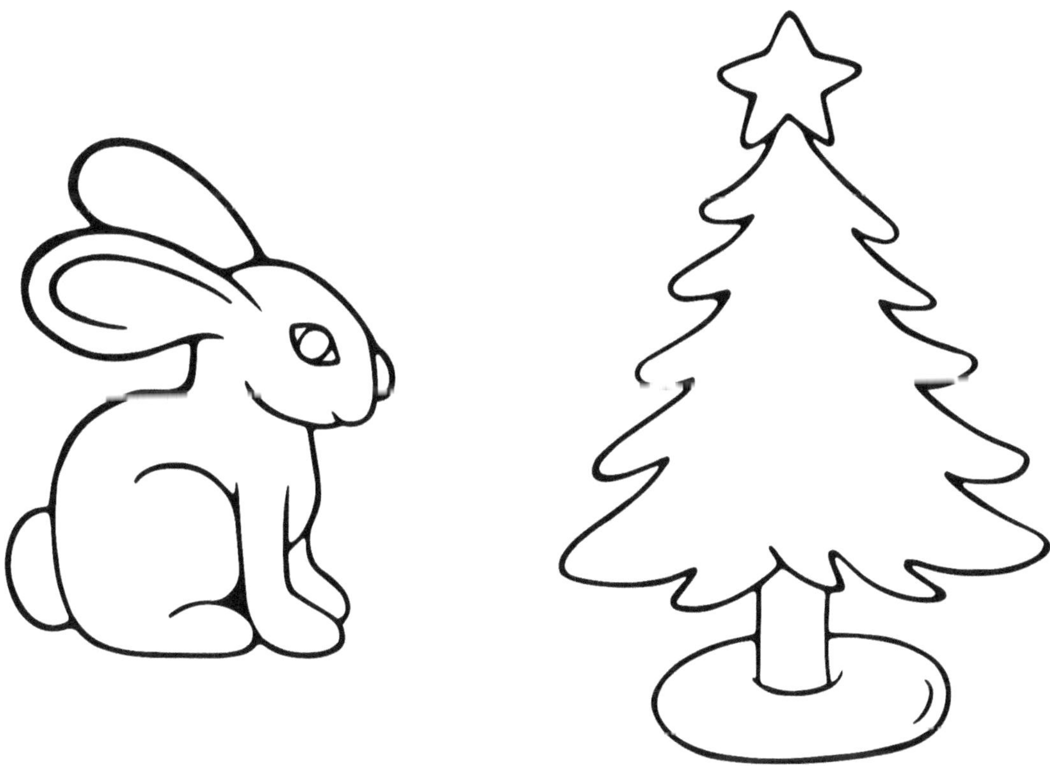

New Years - Memories

1

2

3

4

5

6

7

8

9

10

11

Remembering The Holidays - ArtZillustrations.com

New Years - Memories

1

2

3

4

5

6

7

8

9

10

11

Remembering The Holidays - ArtZillustrations.com

Valentines Day - Memories

1

2

3

4

5

6

7

8

9

10

11

Remembering The Holidays - ArtZillustrations.com

Valentines Day - Memories

1

2

3

4

5

6

7

8

9

10

11

Remembering The Holidays - ArtZillustrations.com

St. Patricks Day - Memories

1

2

3

4

5

6

7

8

9

10

11

Remembering The Holidays - ArtZillustrations.com

St. Patricks Day - Memories

1

2

3

4

5

6

7

8

9

10

11

Remembering The Holidays - ArtZillustrations.com

Easter - Memories

1

2

3

4

5

6

7

8

9

10

11

Remembering The Holidays - ArtZillustrations.com

Easter - Memories

1

2

3

4

5

6

7

8

9

10

11

Remembering The Holidays - ArtZillustrations.com

Memorial Day - Memories

1

2

3

4

5

6

7

8

9

10

11

Memorial Day - Memories

1

2

3

4

5

6

7

8

9

10

11

Remembering The Holidays - ArtZillustrations.com

4th Of July - Memories

1

2

3

4

5

6

7

8

9

10

11

Remembering The Holidays - ArtZillustrations.com

4th Of July - Memories

1

2

3

4

5

6

7

8

9

10

11

Remembering The Holidays - ArtZillustrations.com

Halloween - Memories

1

2

3

4

5

6

7

8

9

10

11

Remembering The Holidays - ArtZillustrations.com

Halloween - Memories

1

2

3

4

5

6

7

8

9

10

11

Remembering The Holidays - ArtZillustrations.com

Thanksgiving - Memories

1

2

3

4

5

6

7

8

9

10

11

Remembering The Holidays - ArtZillustrations.com

Thanksgiving - Memories

1

2

3

4

5

6

7

8

9

10

11

Remembering The Holidays - ArtZillustrations.com

Hanuka - Memories

1

2

3

4

5

6

7

8

9

10

11

Remembering The Holidays - ArtZillustrations.com

Hanuka - Memories

1

2

3

4

5

6

7

8

9

10

11

Remembering The Holidays - ArtZillustrations.com

Christmas - Memories

1

2

3

4

5

6

7

8

9

10

11

Remembering The Holidays - ArtZillustrations.com

Christmas - Memories

1

2

3

4

5

6

7

8

9

10

11

Remembering The Holidays - ArtZillustrations.com

Go To ArtZillustrations.com For More
Interactive Coloring Books, Adult Coloring Books, Journals & Products

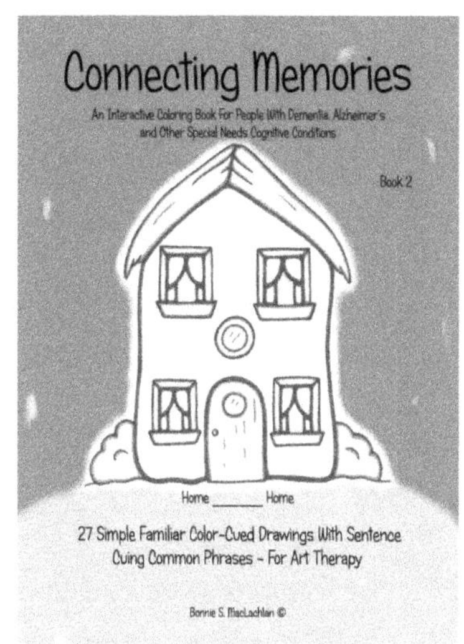

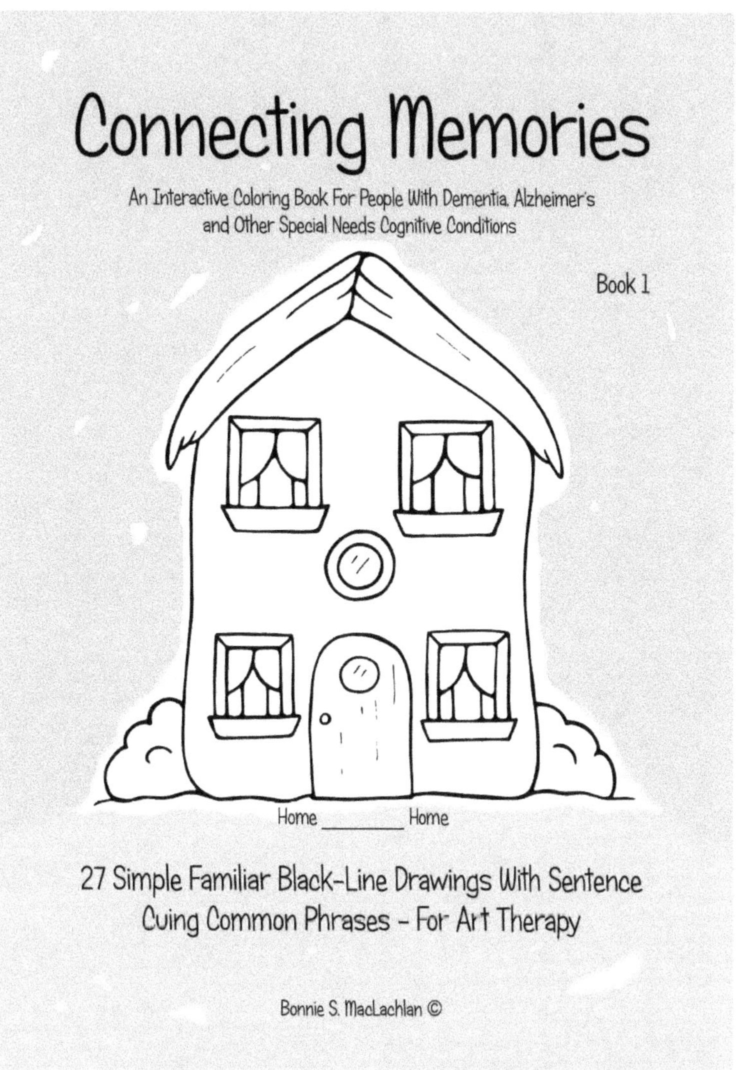

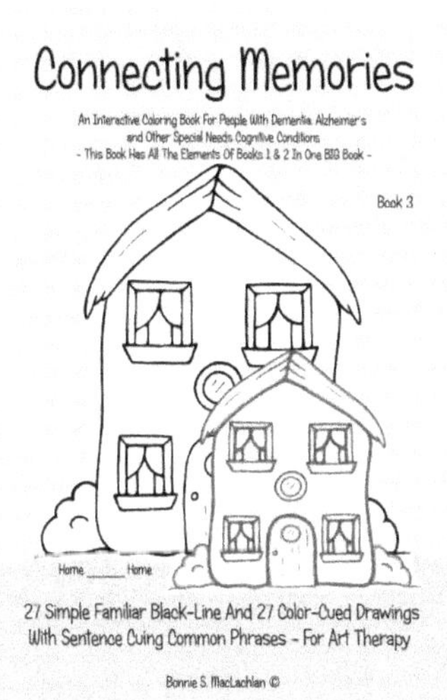

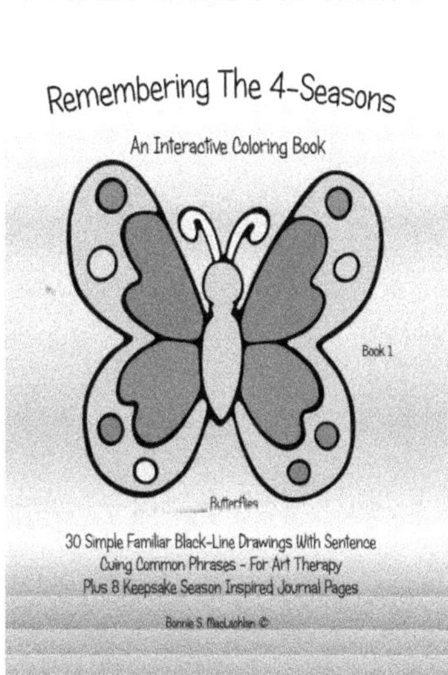

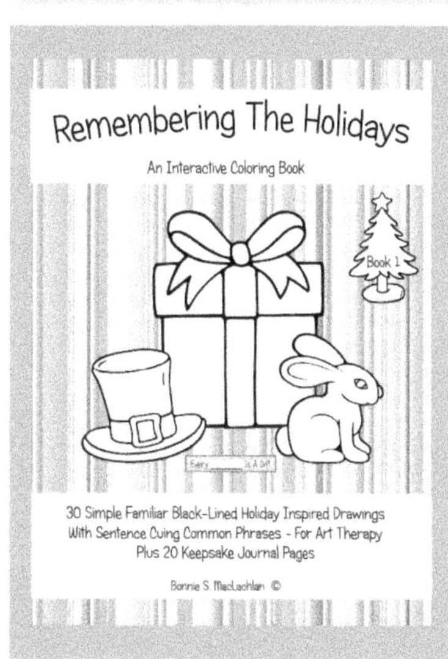

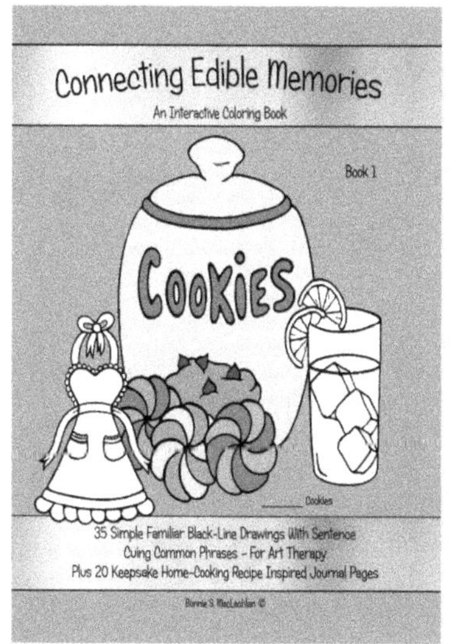

www.ingramcontent.com/pod-product-compliance
Lightning Source LLC
LaVergne TN
LVHW081419110826
845149LV00010B/1796

* 9 7 8 0 9 9 7 7 8 8 9 1 4 *